THE THOMAS KINKADE STORY

AUTUMN SNOW (Published 2000) I heard reports of an early snow east of our home in Placerville. The trees flamed orange and gold in their final blaze of fall color. The new-fallen snow still clung to them, adding winter's glistening white to the glory of autumn. I painted *Autumn Snow* some years ago, and its meaning has deepened for me as I pass through the seasons of my own life.

THE THOMAS KINKADE STORY

A 20-YEAR CHRONOLOGY OF THE ARTIST

THOMAS KINKADE
TEXT BY RICK BARNETT

BULFINCH PRESS
AOL TIME WARNER BOOK GROUP
BOSTON · NEW YORK · LONDON

FIRST EDITION

LIBRARY OF CONGRESS CATALOGING-IN-PUBLICATION DATA
BARNETT, RICK.
    THE THOMAS KINKADE STORY: A 20-YEAR CHRONOLOGY OF THE ARTIST / RICK BARNETT.—1ST ED.
    P. CM.
    ISBN 0-8212-2858-7
    1. KINKADE, THOMAS, 1958- 2. PAINTERS—UNITED STATES—BIOGRAPHY, I. TITLE.
ND237.K535B37 2004
759.13–DC21
[B]
                                                                            2003052256

(SPECIAL EDITION ISBN 0-8212-7753-7)

BULFINCH PRESS IS A DIVISION OF
AOL TIME WARNER BOOK GROUP.

DESIGN BY ERIC BAKER DESIGN

PRINTED IN SPAIN

TO NANETTE

– THOMAS KINKADE

Books have a life of their own. This one is no exception. From an idea that one has, many collaborate to bring the final product to the reader.

Appreciation to the **Thomas Kinkade National Archive** and **Thomas Kinkade Museum**, in Monterey, California. Both have been responsible for much of the historical documentation in this project, without which it would have been a very different book. **George Carpenter** of Placerville along with **Bob and Cathy Adorni** were invaluable resources. In addition, the **Polm Collection** generously surrendered many of its treasures for photographic documentary from the finest collection of Kinkade originals.

Finally, as the book began, God had His purpose. Lori, my wife and gift, provided proof of that throughout the process. Bob and Carolyn, Helga, Sara, and Kristen have all played a role in my special relationship with the artist.

Thomas, Nanette, and the girls gave insight from beginning to end. *The Thomas Kinkade Story* is their gift to you.

– RICK BARNETT

A QUIET EVENING (1998) The heart has its special places: quiet retreats, fragrant with the sweet perfume of flowers, bathed in the romantic light of sunset, soothed by the music of a laughing brook and droning bees. Places made possible by the precious gift of love.

CONTENTS

IN THE BEGINNING

BESIDE STILL WATERS (1993) *Beside Still Waters* is my vision of what the Garden of Eden must have been like. As a Christian, I speculate on the mystery and wonder of God's creation when nature was perfect, unspoiled. As an artist, I try to convey my own wonder at the richness and variety I still find in the natural world.

IN THE BEGINNING

"IN THE BEGINNING…" THE FIRST THREE WORDS OF THE BOOK OF GENESIS MONUMENTALLY PROCLAIM THAT ALL THINGS, OF NECESSITY, MUST HAVE A STARTING POINT. THE SAME ANCIENT SCRIPTURES SAY THAT THE EARTH WAS DARK AND EMPTY AT FIRST, A FORMLESS MASS, AND THEN GOD HIMSELF PROCLAIMED, "LET THERE BE LIGHT," AND THERE WAS LIGHT. THE NEXT VERSE ADDS THAT AFTER CREATING THE LIGHT, GOD SAW THAT IT WAS GOOD — THE FIRST MENTION IN THE BIBLE OF GOD ASSESSING SOMETHING AS GOOD.

Virtually every faith since the beginning of time has embraced light as symbolic of godliness and truth, whereas darkness usually represents ignorance and evil. For Thomas Kinkade, especially in the twenty years he's been publishing art, this spiritual symbolism of light and darkness has always informed, even inspired, his vision as an artist. He freely talks in public lectures and interviews about the goodness of light and of his desire as an artist to impart light to others in both a visual and a spiritual sense.

Kinkade's faith serves both as a source of inspiration to create and a motivation to serve others through what he creates. For him, faith is not a matter of pious rectitude and burdensome pretense, but rather a vibrant, living thing, at once radiant and down-to-earth. In fact, his many public appearances are often punctuated with references to faith, as well as humorous, gently self-deprecating anecdotes. Kinkade is quick to point out his own failings and foibles, and constantly reaffirms that his desire is to have his audience look to his art, rather than to him personally, for inspiration. He frequently makes reference to his belief that the arts can be a form of personal worship, a vital communion with the Creator. As he has stated, "I often feel closest to God as I am painting. I frequently pray for God to use my work to bless the lives of those who see it. To me, if people receive anything good from these paintings, I have to believe it came from God rather than me." Clearly Kinkade, like many in the Western tradition of art, sees himself as an imperfect tool in the hands of an all-perfect God.

Thomas Kinkade poses at the Wallace Road studio, circa 1989

PACIFIC NOCTURNE (circa 1983-1984) Completed in the early 1980s, *Pacific Nocturne* hung in the Kinkade family home as the centerpiece of the artist's personal collection during the Wallace Road era. This romanticized coastal beach scene captures a Mendocino sunset and was painted as a dedication to the couple's second anniversary while Thom and Nanette revisited their honeymoon getaway.

PART I

THE
EARLY
YEARS

The Kinkade family, 2002

WILLIAM THOMAS KINKADE III was born in Sacramento, California, on January 19, 1958. His father, Bill Kinkade, and mother, Mary Anne, were a typical couple of that era. Bill was a World War II veteran and bounced from job to job over the years, while Mary Anne Kinkade worked in various clerical positions to help make ends meet. The family also included Thom's sister, Katherine, seven years his senior, and his younger brother by eighteen months, Patrick. The latter became a childhood "partner in mischief" to young Thom, and to this day they share a robust, if at times highly idiosyncratic, humor.

Five years after Kinkade was born, his family moved to the tiny Sierra foothills village of Latrobe, California. He and Patrick embraced with wide-eyed wonder their new surroundings, exploring the countryside and engaging in fanciful Tom Sawyeresque adventures. Many domestic animals and wild creatures surrounded him, and, as Kinkade remembers it,

"the hills seemed ever so green, with small brooks running down the hillsides and moss-covered rock outcroppings under the spreading oaks." The romantic vision of landscape so central to Kinkade's artistic identity was absorbed during these early years.

Shortly after Kinkade's sixth birthday, his parents suffered an experience all too common with couples of the postwar era — they found themselves facing a failed marriage. Kinkade's father had continued to work in Sacramento after the move to Latrobe, and the strain of the daily commute and separation time finally broke the family apart. Mary Anne took the children and moved to the small gold rush–era town of Placerville, at that time a rural agricultural town, taking up residence in a countryside trailer park. Though struggling to live on Mary Anne's meager income, the family nonetheless flourished. The trailer park, though dilapidated, furnished young Thom with a wealth of wistful memories. "There was a pond there, and my

brother and I used to go fishing with some of the other kids from the park. There was a little country market on the corner of the main road, and we would proudly walk down there, dimes in hand, to purchase bottles of root beer out of the old chest cooler." Kinkade's growing sense of small-town Americana was nourished by the villagelike atmosphere of the tree-shaded trailer park. "It was like a village within a village," Kinkade has said. "Everything was within walking distance and you knew your neighbors."

A year or so later, the family left the trailer park for a series of apartments and eventually settled into a home of their own. Even though Mary Ann had no money for a down payment, the kind-hearted seller of the property allowed the struggling family to move in without putting any money down. She would later deem these circumstances "miraculous."

Kinkade took solace in what was to become his primary medium of self-expression, even self-preservation: drawing. "I always had sketchbooks in my hand from the days of my earliest childhood memories. My mother has told me that I was drawing long before I could walk, and that giving me a crayon was often the only thing that would keep me from fussing as a toddler."

During Kinkade's early school years in Placerville, his talent as an artist began to manifest itself. "I was known as the kid who could draw, and it gave me attention, like any other skill a child might have. My friend Donald could stand on his head; another friend knew how to skip rocks. I could draw." As Kinkade began to get attention for his prodigious talent, he found reinforcement in the audience it gave him. For him, the creative urge seems always to have been linked to a deep-seated need to please, or, to put it in his later Christian parlance, "to serve." "I don't really think that an artist can be entirely self-contained," Kinkade has commented. "Without someone to share the art with, the circle is not complete."

By the fifth grade, Kinkade was drawing obsessively, often selling his drawings (especially caricatures of the less-liked teachers) to

his schoolmates. He began to recognize his art as a means of financial reward, and this instinct toward commerce fueled his creative output. Much like the poor city child who seeks to escape his environment through achievement in sports, Kinkade began to see his artistic talent as a tool for deliverance from the impoverished surroundings of a broken family and a provincial small town. "Art was my handle—a means of self-identity that gave me hope for the future despite the run-down neighborhood I lived in and the sense I had of the limited opportunities available to me," Kinkade has said.

Kinkade was exposed to oil painting for the first time in an accelerated art class during his freshman year in high school. "It was a case of instantaneous love," Kinkade has said. "The moment I took up an oil painting brush for the first time, I felt like I was coming home. I felt strangely as if I instinctually knew how to do this."

That summer, Kinkade had another life-changing encounter. In his role as a hardworking contributor to the family's finances, Kinkade had undertaken a number of youthful enterprises, among them a paper route delivering the *Sacramento Bee* newspaper. One afternoon, as he wended his way through the village lanes of Placerville delivering papers, he encountered an arresting sight.

"It's difficult to imagine the impact the first sight of Nanette had on me," Kinkade has said. "She was standing beside a moving van, her family having just moved into the neighborhood. I was smitten at once!"

Kinkade's friendship with the beautiful blond girl evolved into an innocent childhood romance. They became sweethearts and constant companions, walking hand in hand into town together on Saturday afternoons, spending endless days reading poetry to each other beneath a spreading sycamore tree, even slipping each other secret love notes. (The latter have been saved through the years as treasured family artifacts.)

Nanette Willey had been raised in a family quite different from Kinkade's. Nanette's father, Al Willey, was an inveterate traveler who over the years had sought to expose his young family to different cultures.

"Nanette's family had visited some exotic places," Kinkade remembers. "As she spoke of these adventures, my youthful imagination caught fire. Her family had lived in the Philippines and Japan and had traveled throughout the Far East. Her stories of flying to distant lands aboard bomber planes when her father was employed by a military school intrigued me. I knew that my destiny lay in exploring the world and seeing what lay beyond the horizons of my small-town life."

Nanette was immediately enamored with Thom's humor, intelligence, zest for living, and talent. Her goal was to become a nurse and to have a family, and she and Thom became partners in planning for the life ahead. "Thom and I would talk for hours about what we wanted to do in the future," Nanette has said. "He and

I were always dreaming of our life as a married couple: him painting at the easel, myself working on various projects, and a group of young kids underfoot." Many of those childhood dreams have come true for Thomas and Nanette, perhaps to an extent they would never have dared hope for in those early years.

In 1974, during his second year in high school, Kinkade experienced yet another event of life-changing proportions. "One afternoon, as I was walking down the gravel road that led to our house, I looked across the neighboring field and saw some workmen rebuilding one of the barns on our neighbor's property. Out of curiosity, I walked over and asked them what they were up to and was told that they were converting the barn into an artist's studio. My heart began to pound in my chest. Could it be that I would get a chance to meet a real artist?"

The artist in question was Glenn Wessels, a well-known educator in the arts and famous in his own right as one of the

progenitors, along with Elmer Bischoff, David Park, Richard Diebenkorn, and others, of the Bay Area figurative school. Wessels had retired from a teaching position at the University of California and decided to establish a studio in Placerville after his beloved wife of many years passed away.

The elder artist was approaching his eightieth birthday at the time of his transition to country living, and his physical health was failing. "Glenn had been in a jeep accident with his friend Ansel Adams while they were photographing together in the Sierras," Kinkade remembers. "He needed a walker to get about after that and frequently took naps on the sundeck on lazy summer afternoons to regain his strength. When he began working in the barn studio, I presented myself to him and asked him if he needed help around the studio. He jumped at the chance to have a young assistant around the place. I became his handyman and apprentice for the next three years."

Wessels's vast experience and deep intellect were like streams of refreshing water to the aspiring young artist. Wessels undertook to impart to Kinkade his sixty-plus years of experience as an artist, educator, world traveler, and distinguished critic and writer. "Glenn Wessels became a father figure to me," Kinkade has said. "I would sit beside him in his studio as he end-lessly reminisced about his adventures in Paris between the world wars, his friendships with Picasso, Ernest Hemingway, Gertrude Stein, and other luminaries of that era. Glenn had been a great world traveler and spoke lovingly of his deceased wife, who had been his constant companion for many decades. He had photo albums filled with tattered black-and-white shots of him and his wife cross-country skiing through the Alps or painting on the streets of Paris. It filled me with a romance for that kind of life, and I think Nanette and I have sought to emulate this adventuresome artist's life in our own fashion."

Wessels was also a deep thinker, and he encouraged Kinkade to study broadly in many fields. He viewed the artist's life as a high calling, almost a form of priesthood, that entailed complete devo-tion. "To Glenn, being an artist was all-consuming — a lifetime commitment to explore and record the world around us," says Kinkade. "In all his countless hours of teaching me and molding my character, I was impressed with his constant admonishment regarding 'passion.' Like Auntie Mame, he viewed life as a great banquet that needed to be tasted broadly. He often encouraged me to never let the conventions of our culture limit my curios-ity about the full range of human experience. I think to this day that my fascination with the diversity of life and my passion to make the most of every minute stem in part from the encouragement given me by Wessels."

One more practical aspect of Wessels's influence was his insistence that Kinkade undertake studies at the University of

OLD WATCHMAKER (pre-1982)
Kinkade captures the master craftsman in this oil. The watchmaker, in his twilight years, seems to be viewing the newly completed timepiece and reflecting on the learned skill that perhaps became extinct with his generation.

California at Berkeley. As a professor emeritus of that respected institution, Wessels introduced Kinkade to faculty members during a two-day visit to the campus in 1976. Wessels believed that Kinkade would be exposed to the most diverse group of students and faculty at the Berkeley campus and that he would encounter great minds there. The intellectual environment, combined with the pluralistic culture, was the perfect mix, Wessels reasoned, for this enthusiastic and intellectually curious young artist emerging from a typical American small town.

In the fall of 1976, Kinkade began studies at the University of California at Berkeley and immediately flourished. By chance, Kinkade's roommate was another young artist, James Gurney, who went on to create *Dinotopia*. The two became fast friends and sketching companions, encouraging each other to develop new techniques and to spare no effort in pursuing their devotion to art. Kinkade and Gurney shared a hunger for adventure and began plotting ways in which to explore the world around them. Their common humor lent itself to elaborate stunts and pranks engineered by the pair, much to the disdain of other members of the college community. Their stunts involved masks, slapstick antics, and the like, and a sense of good-humored mayhem was a constant undercurrent of their companionship.

During his freshman year at college, Kinkade undertook to create a studio for himself in the basement of the shabby student apartment building where he lived. As he remembers it, "The room was about twenty feet square and had large pipes running through the ceiling. The space was damp and dark, and I had the feeling of being cloistered in a private cell with nothing to interrupt my work. During this phase, I created elaborate tableaux of still-life objects, which I rendered in great detail, as well as portraits of my friends. I also honed my skills by constantly painting outdoors." During the Berkeley years, this latter pursuit began emerging as a distinct emphasis in Kinkade's creative life. Kinkade's devotion to outdoor painting had begun in his early years while at an art camp in the Sierra Nevadas. Throughout high school he continued the habit of taking his paints into natural settings and recording what he saw. By the time he reached Berkeley, this practice had become such an obsession that he frequently planned painting trips to the Sierras, the Central Valley of California, San Francisco, and other scenic areas.

Kinkade's Berkeley studio became a refuge from his studies when he found his interest in academia waning as his desire to paint increased. Though he was an avid reader and interested in a broad range of topics, Kinkade's taste for scholastic achievement was mitigated by his growing artistic identity. After two years of intense study at Berkeley, Kinkade headed south to the Art Center College of Design in Pasadena, California, to focus on developing his painting skills. His friend Gurney soon joined him there, and they became neighbors at the Golden Palms, a ghetto apartment complex in East Los Angeles.

"The Golden Palms was an atmosphere of creative activity unparalleled in my experience to that time," Kinkade has commented. "Almost everyone who lived there then was an art student, and the camaraderie was intense. We would have impromptu sketching sessions day and night and would share ideas about composition and technique. All of us were working hard at Art Center, and the enthusiasm was contagious." His roommate during this time was Paul Chadwick, who later became famous as the creator of a comic-book icon called Concrete. Other members of the Golden Palms circle included Ron Harris and Bryn Barnard, both destined to become well-known illustrators, as well as other individuals who later became established film directors, screenwriters, and graphic artists of every description. There was a great deal of energy generated by

YOSEMITE MEADOWS (1983) Kinkade was moved by a series of trips taken through Wyoming, Montana, and the Sierras. This piece highlights the influence that Thomas found as he discovered the Charles Russell Museum and Yosemite, bringing forth the American Indian's nineteenth-century life.

the Golden Palms circle, and Kinkade's art was invigorated to new levels during this phase.

During these formative years, Kinkade remembers being torn between his desire to pursue his personal vision as an artist and the urge for commercial success. To many of his colleagues, this conflict presented no dilemma. "Of necessity many of the Art Center students focused on the goal of making a living from their talent," Kinkade says. "I certainly shared that goal, but I also felt some deeper sense of mission — the desire to make a difference in the world with whatever talent I had. Perhaps it was all that training from Glenn Wessels."

Kinkade pursued his vision by showing his paintings in galleries in the Los Angeles area while still an art student. He was pleasantly surprised to discover that the paintings met with immediate success. At this time he was creating highly romantic landscape paintings, influenced by the epic painters of the American tradition. "I was very influenced by the Hudson River School

painters. While I was a student at Berkeley, I had discovered Thomas Hill, Albert Bierstadt, and other monumental-landscape painters. The tradition of landscape painting in America as an expression of idealism and spiritual revelry intrigued me," Kinkade remembers.

After their second year at Art Center, Kinkade and Gurney embarked on a whirlwind trip across America aboard boxcars. Their adventures as "hobo artists" were eventually recorded in their book, *The Artist's Guide to Sketching*. The trip confirmed Kinkade's passion for adventure and for working on the spot. Returning from their exploits, the pair left their studies at Art Center to finish the manuscript for the book. But there was a problem: They needed to find a way to pay their bills as they worked on the project. To remedy the situation, both Kinkade and Gurney sought employment in the movie industry and were eventually hired by director Ralph Bakshi, who was beginning work on an animated film entitled *Fire and Ice*. This relatively big-budget production was inspired by the fantasy imagery of legendary illustrator Frank Frazetta.

Frazetta became yet another artistic mentor to Kinkade during his years working on the movie. "Frank would often wander into the studio and ruminate on some aspect or another of his life. He was an amazingly talented man, and I identified with the deep delight he felt for life and painting," Kinkade says. Kinkade's work on *Fire and Ice* involved extensive use of artistic imagination. The worlds depicted in the film were not real places but fanciful, dreamlike settings. "You had to rely on your creativity for every painting you worked on," Kinkade remembers. "There was no way to go out and photograph an ice crystal palace or a subterranean world filled with bubbling lakes of fire. So you had to make it up as you went. I think that experience was invaluable in my future work, since most of what I create today is highly imaginative."

Meanwhile, his paintings continued to be popular at galleries, and Kinkade's newfound financial stability emboldened him to seek out his childhood sweetheart, Nanette Willey, and establish a

family. In what he describes as "one of the most fundamental miracles of my life," Kinkade woke up one morning having had a vivid dream that he reunited with Nanette. Kinkade immediately phoned her, and the two entered an exhilarating phase of long-distance dating, with Kinkade often driving twelve hours at a time after work to spend a precious Sunday with his beloved Nanette and returning exhausted after an all-night driving stint to resume work on Monday.

In 1980 or so, Kinkade experienced what he later referred to as "an amazing touch of God's mercy and love" during an old-fashioned tent crusade in Southern California. From that point onward, Kinkade viewed his life and work in terms of his faith, and his talent as a tool for personal ministry. To this day, he maintains that the real products of his paintbrush are hope, peace, and love, as embodied in imagery shared with others through paintings, prints, and assorted products.

As the production of *Fire and Ice* was winding down, Kinkade and Nanette were married on May 2, 1982, and soon after returned to their childhood home of Placerville. They moved to a ranch region north of town and established their home on a ten-acre parcel that featured an old barn. The barn was quickly converted into a studio, and Kinkade entered an era of great productivity. In 1983, the young couple pursued a dream that had long been forming in Kinkade's heart: to publish prints of Kinkade's luminous landscape paintings. "My work was selling so well that creating prints seemed like a natural extension of my artistic productivity. This was also consistent with my personal mission of sharing inspiration with others through my art," Kinkade remembers. "Nanette and I took our life savings and printed our first limited edition. We held our breath and prayed it would be successful." That prayer was apparently answered. In fact, Kinkade's first few prints quickly sold out, and with the funds from the endeavor, Kinkade began publishing more prints.

Following this initial success in publishing, Kinkade began to see the business viability of fine art distribution. With friend and coentrepreneur Ken Raasch, he envisioned a full-fledged company devoted to the distribution of his artwork. "Ken and I got together and laid the plans for what would become Lightpost Publishing sometime in the late eighties. The company grew slowly at first and then seemed to reach a point of critical mass and almost exploded. At times, we felt we were on a roller coaster, hanging on for the ride. In retrospect, I can see God's hand was guiding every step of the way, but at the time the growth seemed overwhelming."

PLACERVILLE, MAIN STREET, 1916 (1984)

PART II

20 YEARS OF

PUBLISHED WORK

DAWSON (1984) This work shows the famous Yukon town of Dawson during the height of the northern gold rush, around 1898. The era I depicted in *Dawson* must have been brutal indeed. Yet, with the hardships of survival comes the exuberance of camaraderie.

1984-1989

IN 1984, THOMAS AND NANETTE celebrated their second wedding anniversary with a return trip to Mendocino, California. Shortly thereafter, the Kinkades decided to leave Southern California, returning to Placerville to start a family. The house on Wallace Road in his hometown of Placerville became the birthing place of Kinkade's new work and his future as a published artist.

Once again, Thom's entrepreneurial spirit combined with his desire to do good. The El Dorado County Friends of the Library needed to raise funds for a new library building and Thomas Kinkade was ready with a fresh idea. He created a turn-of-the-century portrait of a California gold rush town entitled *Placerville, Main Street, 1916*, with proceeds from the sale of prints going to the library. Original prints sold for under fifty dollars.

Energized by his new venture, Kinkade traveled to Alaska, exploring the wilderness and historic old villages via floatplane. The "Dawson Series" resulted: three paintings — *Dawson* (page 28), *Birth of a City* (page 30), and *Moonlight on the Riverfront* (not shown) — each released as a limited-edition print.

Kinkade's work flourished in gallery exhibits in Carmel, Los Angeles, and San Francisco. With his style identified, collectors looking with a discerning eye for the next undiscovered Parrish or Rockwell zeroed in on his work. Exhibit brochures, once used to entice purchasers to attend a showing of the artist's work, created

BIRTH OF A CITY (1985, Published 1990)

sellouts of the art before the event! Kinkade needed to complete new works in secret, bringing them to shows so that the gallery had artwork to sell during the artist's appearance.

Nineteen eighty-four was the foundation of what became Kinkade's legacy of early works. Evolving forward, 1989 would bring a new style, catapulting him to national fame. Some original works created during this era were released during the next two decades in limited-edition form.

"Frozen Dawn" 18x24

Thomas Kinkade's paintings exhibit a timelessness and tranquility that align them with the 19th century tradition of romantic landscape painting. Born in Sacramento, California in 1958, he matured early as an artist, partly as a result of a childhood spent sketching the beauty of his native Sierras. His formal education began at the University of California, Berkeley and continued at the Art Center College of Design in Los Angeles.

His love of sketching led to another project. In 1982, he and partner James Gurney traveled across the United States sketching and developing the idea for a book. It was subsequently published by Watson-Guptill as "A Guide to Sketching," and has been highly successful. Kinkade has for the past few years concentrated entirely on pursuing his vision as a landscape painter. He has had several successful shows, including a two-man show in 1983 with Michael Coleman at the C. M. Russell Museum in Montana.

Kinkade lives on a small ranch near his hometown in Northern California. He and his wife Nannette continue to explore the Sierras and the great Northwest. A recent expedition took him by bush plane into the Alaskan interior to sketch desolate mountains and valleys rarely seen by artists.

Mr. & Mrs. Douglas M. Jones
take great pleasure in inviting you
to preview
a major exhibition for

THOMAS KINKADE

Thursday, May 31st   5:30-8:00 pm
Mr. Kinkade will be present

Cocktails will be served
Valet Parking

The Show will continue thru June

The JONES GALLERY

1264 Prospect Street, La Jolla, California 92037   (619) 459-1370

"The Monarch" 20x16

SAN FRANCISCO, 1909 (1985) You can almost smell the salt air, hear the clanging trolleys and shouts of vendors – so great is the vastness and vitality of *San Francisco, 1909*.

PASSING STORM, NORTHERN ROCKIES (1986)

CLEARING SKIES (1984)

RANGE OF LIGHT (1984)

MORNING MIST (1987)

NEW YORK, CENTRAL PARK SOUTH AT SIXTH AVENUE (1986) This corner typifies the ebullience and energy that is New York at its best. I've tried to capture the motion of the street in this canvas, one of my earliest efforts depicting a city setting.

MAIN STREET COURTHOUSE (Published 1995) Main Street is a place we, as children, would go to on Saturdays aboard bicycles that nearly flew as we pedaled down the dusty city streets toward our destination.

MAIN STREET CELEBRATION (Published 1995) Main Street! This is the place where people gather to do their business and share the activities of a simpler era; I hope you'll meet me on Main Street!

MAIN STREET TROLLEY (Published 1995) In my Main Street Memories collection, I share the Main Streets of my imagination — places where trolley cars clang and a celebration is always in progress.

MAIN STREET MATINEE (Published 1995) Main Street was for me a dreamy, idyllic destination, like some foreign country that one reads of and thinks of often, but rarely gets to visit.

WINTER GLEN (Published 1999) One of the most thoroughgoing of my Impressionist experiments, *Winter Glen* displays snow-laden boughs defined by patterns of light and shade; their shadows dance on the brilliantly lit path. *Winter Glen* remains one of my favorites.

BLOCK ISLAND (Published 1998) I love lighthouses. The severe, uncompromising lives of service lived by lonely lighthouse keepers possess a special dignity. The lighthouse has become a profound symbol of human life, poised as it is between the transitory and the eternal.

LINGERING DUSK (Published 1998) I discovered some of my most favorite subjects early on in my career — majestic mountains bathed in the dramatic light of sunset, humble homes nestled in a tranquil natural setting. They're all here in *Lingering Dusk*.

WINTER CHAPEL (Published 1999) I dearly love the mountains. I like to think of them as God's cathedrals. When men build a modest chapel under the soaring peaks, the setting takes on a sacred serenity. *Winter Chapel* portrays just such a scene.

DAYS OF PEACE (Published 1994) *Days of Peace,* painted in the mid 1980s, is typical of my work on the theme of the American Indians. The looming mountain resembles those I've seen in the Cascades and Rockies; its massive presence is echoed by the teepees in the foreground.

CREEKSIDE TRAIL (Published 1994) In *Creekside Trail,* the Redwoods guard the tranquility of a hidden bower, where stream, trail, and a grove of flaming bushes come together in perfect harmony. The setting sun is a masterful painter, touching leaf and water with a radiance that awakens colors that were once concealed.

DUSK IN THE VALLEY (Published 1994) In *Dusk in the Valley,* a peaceful, fertile farm is guarded by great mountain peaks. The scene is not all tranquility; there is drama and energy, courtesy of a blazing golden sunset that seems almost like a celestial spotlight shining down from the heavens.

SPRING IN THE ALPS (Published 1994)
Spring in the Alps fondly recalls a maiden voyage to the Alps in 1985. A great peak, perhaps the famed Jungfrau, lends its snow-clad dignity to *Spring in the Alps,* while delicate alpine flowers bloom and trees stand as silent sentinels.

TWILIGHT VISTA (Published 1999) In this dramatic mountainscape, jagged clouds rise above the snowcapped mountains, forming a ghostly second range that towers heavenward. In the radiant twilight, the texture of cloud is only marginally different from the texture of rock. Both are majestic.

WINTER'S END (Published 1993) *Winter's End* is about that special time when winter warms into spring. It's also about the tracks we leave in our passage through life. I like to imagine that the sled that left its trail in the melting snow might be the same one that carried the traveler in Robert Frost's famous poem.

WINTER LIGHT (Published 1998) The blizzard has passed, covering the earth with a blanket of snow. The spirit of nature is alive and thriving in *Winter Light*. Evergreens stand strong, stoic under the weight of the heavy winter frost, while bright rays from the returning sun reflect and shine — a warming glow that reminds us of His presence.

ENTRANCE TO THE MANOR HOUSE (Published 1990) *Lord of the manor* — I just love the sense of tradition behind those words. The title conveys a sense of domain and dignity that seems very British to me.

TOWN SQUARE (Published 1999) Most of our lives are lived in the company of friends and neighbors. There is a pleasure to cities and to rural retreats, but no habitation seems quite so comfortable to me as the town square.

CHRISTMAS AT THE COURTHOUSE (Published 1990)   During the bustling holiday season, evenings downtown are full of glitter, lights, music, and people bursting with excitement over the joyous time that is upon them. The courthouse, which during any other time of year is a focal point within this small town, is now overshadowed by the beauty of the marvelous tree.

YOSEMITE VALLEY, LATE AFTERNOON LIGHT AT ARTIST'S POINT (1989, Published 1992) This painting depicts the Yosemite Valley as seen from a little-known place called Artist's Point, named in tribute to the many nineteenth-century artists who favored it as a sketching ground. In 1989, the National Park System selected *Yosemite Valley* as its official print.

1989-1993

BY THE EARLY 1990S Kinkade's trademark style began to emerge. His interest in epic landscape had fused with the influence of his extensive travels in Europe, especially in England, and a more intimate viewpoint began to emerge. Light became important to Kinkade's artistic vision, not only as an expression of visual contrast and luminous color but also as a tool to suggest spiritual values within a painting. "I began to see that something consistent was happening in my paintings," says Kinkade. "Every scene I envisioned was constructed to enhance a sense of radiant light. I was influenced at this time by the American luminists, the Dutch light painters of the seventeenth century, and others who utilized light in a spiritual way. I began to see that all of Western painting up through the impressionists was fundamentally an attempt to capture the effects of light on canvas. It was a moment of deep revelation to me — I suddenly knew I wanted to attempt to use light in new and exciting ways in my work. That vision hasn't changed to this day."

Happily settled in the Sierra foothills of Northern California, Thom and Nanette began a family with the birth of their daughters: first Merritt, followed by Chandler three years later.

Nineteen eighty-nine initiated a definite second phase in Kinkade's artistic evolution. He submitted *Yosemite, Late Afternoon Light at Artist's Point* to the judging committee for the Arts for the Parks national awards. The piece won the Founder's Favorite award and was reproduced on a rare ten-dollar collectors' stamp. Four epic works followed: groundbreaking city scenes of Carmel, New York, and San Francisco, and *Moonlit Village*, featuring a spectacular snow-capped chapel in a mountain village in West Virginia. These timeless images by the artist worked their way through what became a network of galleries throughout America, becoming the launch of Thomas Kinkade.

Thom, Nanette, and the girls had a three-month painting holiday in England at the end of 1990. Thom concentrated on painting English cottages and landscapes of the English countryside. This subject matter proved so popular in galleries, always on the lookout for potential bestselling subject matter, that Kinkade was quickly deluged with requests for English countryside compositions. The series' success was amplified with the introduction of oil highlighting on the canvas print images, which gave them an original-painting look. The frenzy began with *Merritt's Cottage,* continued with *Hidden Cottage,* and peaked with the publication of the iconic *Chandler's Cottage.* The latter image became the inspiration for the artist's licensed-product launch, which included greeting cards from Hallmark, fine-quality porcelain from Bradford, and eventually a community of Kinkade-inspired homes.

By 1992, three galleries representing the artist exclusively had opened in Northern California. A fourth gallery opened in 1993 in Kennebunkport, Maine. This rate of gallery openings seemed ambitious at the time, but within a few short years, Kinkade galleries would exist in every state. Thom's work was acquired by people who had never bought art before — and its appeal extended to collectors of all ages. Art lovers from seventeen to seventy began to seek out the Kinkade experience at their nearest gallery.

Collectors went beyond appreciation of the work's execution and sought out the meaning and motivation behind the art from the artist. What, where, when, and why? People wanted answers, and gallery owners began to uncover intriguing facts and the inspiration behind each piece as they examined the works. Hidden *N*s, a tribute to Nanette, became the Kinkade version of the *Nina*s in Al Hirschfeld's Broadway caricatures.

Family members and friends were the subjects of cameo portraits in many of Thom's works. Kinkade became a storyteller through his paintings, and by the public's rating, he delivered the equivalent of

CARMEL, OCEAN AVENUE ON A RAINY AFTERNOON (1989) Carmel has been a favorite family retreat for many years, so naturally I was excited to finally put on canvas some of my personal feelings about the area. I chose the corner that affords a broad panorama of the characteristics that make Carmel picturesque: Monterey pine trees, flowering hedges, and charming architecture.

MOONLIT VILLAGE (1989) In my travels throughout America I've noticed that churches are often built on a hillside or knoll as a means of emphasizing their presence in a town — I find this to be a particularly poignant concept.

UNION SQUARE, SAN FRANCISCO (Plein Air, Published circa 1998) San Francisco is truly a fascinating place. The hustle and bustle of the city streets combined with the romantic, serene waterfront make this city a favorite subject to paint. Union Square seemed particularly alive on this day, with brilliant light reflecting off the towering buildings and seagulls passing overhead. (Thomas Kinkade completed the studio work of *San Francisco, Late Afternoon at Union Square* in 1989.)

NEW YORK, SNOW ON SEVENTH AVENUE, 1932 (1989) For the most part, I paint places I can see and experience firsthand, though occasionally I enjoy the challenge of creating a romantic vision of another era. I have tried to capture the bustling activity of New York in the twenties and early thirties in *New York, Snow on Seventh Avenue, 1932.*

CHANDLER'S COTTAGE (1990) I've been on the lookout for cottages that would make perfect dream dollhouses for my girls. How Chandler would love to have a real miniature version of this delightful flower-bedecked hutch, complete with blooming garden, in her playroom.

EVENING AT MERRITT'S COTTAGE (1990) My daughter Merritt loves sunsets. So, of course, when on the lookout for Merritt's dream cottage, I paid particular attention to sunset. This house comes alive in the warm glow of dusk, just the way my oldest daughter does.

HIDDEN COTTAGE (1990) *Hidden Cottage* is composed of equal measures of dreams and memories. Once discovered and painted, it is a treasure for all to share.

CHRISTMAS COTTAGE (1990) The Christmas season has always been my favorite time of year. I enjoy the crisp mornings, strands of colored lights, and the feeling of hearth and home. The Christmas Cottage collection is my way of annually celebrating, in paint, the season I most love.

SAN FRANCISCO, A VIEW DOWN CALIFORNIA STREET FROM NOB HILL (1992) I was recently talking to a friend who had relocated near San Francisco and who had never before been to that city. The lights, the mood, the flying flags, and the windswept wisps of fog, the bustling people and the quaint bits of architecture that are San Francisco can't adequately be put into words.

A close-up of Norman Rockwell taken
from **VICTORIAN CHRISTMAS** (1992)

a *New York Times* bestseller with every new release. Kinkade continued to seek out the inspiration of other artists he admired. He painted at Norman Rockwell's celebrated studio in Arlington, Vermont, and also set up his easel in front of Beatrix Potter's cottage in the Lake District of England. Fellowship with these artistic giants produced masterworks of theme, color, depth, and light.

The painting *San Francisco, A View Down California Street From Nob Hill*, arguably Kinkade's most significant early masterwork, was completed in 1992. Never one to be complacent, the artist continued in 1993 with his finest work to date, painting gardens (*Beside Still Waters,* page 8), Victorian houses (*Amber Afternoon*, page 89), and wilderness cabins (*End of a Perfect Day 2*, page 65) as well as cottages, chapels, and city scenes.

The American people and the gallery community embraced Kinkade and his work as if he were a bestselling author or a gold record musician. Within five years of publishing his first print, Thomas Kinkade was a national artistic phenomenon. Further, Kinkade's range of subject matter and color palettes continued to expand.

BOSTON, AN EVENING STROLL THROUGH THE COMMON (1991) Boston is a city for walking! A wet storm front was breaking up overhead one chilly evening when I got the inspiration for this painting. The sweet, warm fragrance of candied peanuts roasting in the sidewalk-vendor's cart and the glowing lights make Boston one of my favorite subjects to paint.

SKATING IN THE PARK (1989) One brisk January evening, Nanette and I were enjoying a romantic ride in a hansom cab through New York's Central Park. As we rounded a brightly lit bend, the cabby stopped and announced, "There she is, Wollman Rink."

PARIS, CITY OF LIGHTS (1993) My *Paris, City of Lights* could be titled *The Kinkade Family in Paris*. I've set the time machine back a few decades and included myself (in the red beret), painting the fabulous Café Nanette. The real Nanette, holding baby Chandler, hails a cab, while our oldest daughter, Merritt, looks on.

FISHERMAN'S WHARF, SAN FRANCISCO (1993) A luminous sunset bathes *Fisherman's Wharf* in a golden glow. Quaint fishing boats of all descriptions sleep quietly at their moorings, and overhead, seagulls soar in the brisk sea air. What an enchanting location!

THE END OF A PERFECT DAY (1993) Paintings like *The End of a Perfect Day* express my growing appreciation for the real beauty of nature untamed. This rustic stone cabin is nestled in a glorious setting — a secluded jewel of a lake framed by distant mountains. It is my ideal place to end a perfect day.

SPRING AT STONEGATE (1990) While strolling with Nanette through the English countryside, I happened upon this magnificent stone cottage nestled among trees and a lavish garden. The contrast between stone and flower, between the obdurate rock and the sensitive plant, the enduring and the evanescent, is at the heart of *Spring at Stonegate*.

GLORY OF WINTER (1993) This is a thrilling view of Bridal Veil Fall, thundering at the head of a Yosemite Valley blanketed in snow and blessed by an unaccustomed solitude. A brilliant beam of sunlight has broken through the clouds, illuminating the distant falls and mountains as if in a spotlight.

MORNING LIGHT (1990) In *Morning Light,* a flower garden becomes a fabulous canvas onto which the sun paints a glowing picture. Suffused through the mist, the light dazzles with subtle flashes of color.

THE BLUE COTTAGE (1990) My English cottage paintings have always been an attempt to reach into the deepest part of my emotions—those hidden joyous fantasies we all have of places more special than our everyday world.

THE WOODSMAN'S THATCH (1991) Though born of the imagination, *The Woodsman's Thatch* is based on real cottages I've sketched during my travels in England. As I worked on this painting, I wanted to enhance the feeling of coziness that seems to be the central mood, so I added a misty rain to lend softness and charm.

CEDAR NOOK COTTAGE (1991) If this seems to you the kind of cottage that Hansel and Gretel might have visited, you're not too far off. Apart from changing the national origin and a few architectural details, this may well pass as a "gingerbread cottage."

CHRISTMAS EVE (1991) *Christmas Eve* is plain and simple, an expression of my ongoing love affair with the Christmas season. This wonderful old stone cottage allows me to express the light, mood, and magic of one of the most wonderful times of the year.

THE LIT PATH (1991) Lights are always a favorite subject of mine, especially when they seem to call me toward a cozy setting. The lights along this walkway not only beckon but also illuminate the way, which is especially helpful for steps that, in typical English fashion, seem as irregular as the ground they cover.

HOME FOR THE EVENING (1991) The title for this tiny painting was originally *Cookies Baking*. As I worked on the piece, I could almost smell the sweet aroma of homemade cookies coming from inside the snow-covered cottage.

OPEN GATE, SUSSEX (1991) Open gates are an invitation to visit, especially when lights glow warmly within an English cottage beyond them. If you're in the mood to chat, you might wander up the rutted lane and knock briskly on the old, weather-worn door of the charming home.

MCKENNA'S COTTAGE (1991) There seems to be a quiet stateliness to classic English cottages such as *McKenna's Cottage*. Every stone seems placed by hand, every bit of thatch carefully bound in place—a patient labor of love.

HOME FOR THE HOLIDAYS (1991) *Home for the Holidays* is an example of memory and imagination blending together to create an idyllic vision. Who hasn't daydreamed about taking a frosty sleigh ride to visit friends for a bit of Christmas Eve cheer?

OLDE PORTERFIELD TEA ROOM (1991) Although the Olde Porterfield Tea Room is imaginary, it is based on those wonderful tea rooms that, along with pubs, seem to be the social center of every English country village.

OLDE PORTERFIELD GIFT SHOPPE (1991) Falling snow brings a hush over the landscape; it's as though the whole world has taken a deep breath in anticipation of some magical moment. In this scene, I enjoyed trying to capture the silent softness of the snow as it blankets the English countryside.

PYE CORNER COTTAGE (1991) The English Pye Corner Cottage is a place where neighbors and travelers meet and friendships are built. And once you've visited Pye Corner Cottage, like the geese in the yard, you will be drawn there for the evening again and again.

THE ROSE ARBOR COTTAGE (1990) Lush roses blossom before a lovely half-hidden cottage—a secluded and most romantic spot. If roses are the emblems of love, then they have designated this as an ideal hideaway for young lovers.

HOME IS WHERE THE HEART IS (1992) As I worked on this painting, I imagined my own family living in this beautiful setting, with wicker chairs for my wife, Nanette, a swing for my three-year-old daughter, Merritt, and even a teddy bear beneath the tree for my younger daughter Chandler!

BLOSSOM HILL CHURCH (1992) This painting is the first piece in my Country Church collection. I have a fondness for all country churches. I'm particularly attached to Blossom Hill Church, since within its weathered walls my wife and I were wed!

CARMEL, DOLORES STREET AND THE TUCK BOX TEA ROOM (1991) Besides the Tuck Box Tea Room, famous for delicious English scones, Dolores Street features many other Carmel landmarks that make for a charming stroll on a rainy afternoon. I hope this Carmel painting will bring a bit of the charm and energy of one of America's most quaint villages to people everywhere!

CHRISTMAS AT THE AHWANEE (1992) I can't think of a better place to celebrate our Savior's birth than Yosemite Valley, one of God's most awesome creations. The Ahwahnee Hotel is located in the heart of the valley and has been there for nearly one hundred years.

COTTAGE BY THE SEA (1992) Though this cottage doesn't exist anywhere but in my painting, I think for many of us it represents an ideal seaside getaway. Of course, I had to paint the scene at sunset. After all, what would a seaside cottage be without a beautiful sunset to watch?

COUNTRY MEMORIES (1992) While visiting New England, Nanette and I decided to search for some of the old haunts of our mutual hero, Norman Rockwell. *Country Memories* is a loving tribute to the charming country area Rockwell called home for so many years.

EVENING CAROLERS (1992) This painting celebrates a universal Christmas tradition: the singing of joyous Christmas carols. There's nothing that lifts the spirit like joining in song with those you love on a crisp December evening!

THE GARDEN PARTY (1992) I discovered this greenhouse in a lush garden within an immense country estate in England. It was great fun painting the costumes of the Victorian era and attempting to capture on canvas the motion and color of a turn-of-the-century garden party!

SUNDAY AT APPLE HILL (1992) Perhaps for as long as there have been Sunday afternoons, there have been Sunday afternoon drives. In the spring, I enjoy packing up the family car after our Sunday worship at church and wandering about in search of wildflowers and picnic spots.

JULIANNE'S COTTAGE (1992) While visiting England one fall, Nanette and I stayed in this cottage; interestingly enough, it was once owned by Beatrix Potter, the renowned creator of Peter Rabbit. By the way, the room we stayed in is the one at the upper left of the cottage.

THE MILLER'S COTTAGE, THOMASHIRE (1992) This painting was executed directly from life, with my easel planted precariously in the mud surrounding the ancient millpond. As I sat observing the tranquil scene, I was amazed at how many people would visit the pond to throw bread and biscuits to the ducks and geese.

MOONLIT SLEIGH RIDE (1992) After a cross-country skiing trip through a snowy valley by moonlight, I decided to paint a tribute to this romantic adventure, with the exception of the skis. Instead, a nostalgic sleigh whisks through the moonlit forest.

VICTORIAN EVENING (1990) Victorian houses are like old friends—they always seem to welcome your visit! This Victorian house is based on a beautiful structure I observed in rural Connecticut.

THE AUTUMN GATE (1991) A gate is an invitation to explore! I spotted this gate while driving through a tiny Cotswold village, having just painted *McKenna's Cottage*. I knew at once I must record the gate in paint, yet since daylight was escaping, I quickly snapped a few reference photos and vowed to re-create the scene in my studio.

SILENT NIGHT (1992) I was so taken with the simple message of the classic Christmas carol "Silent Night," with its images of sleeping villages and the coming of the Christ child, that I decided to give the annual Christmas release the same title and evoke a bit of the song's mood.

SWEETHEART COTTAGE I (1992) Perhaps my sentimental Irish nature is shining through, but I happen to be enchanted with the idea of a romantic hideaway hidden amid blossoming flowers. *Sweetheart Cottage* is a dual tribute to my tenth wedding anniversary and to the most romantic occasion of the year: Valentine's Day.

SKATER'S POND (1993) In *Skater's Pond,* townsfolk have joined together for an evening of skating under the glow of the Christmas tree. I like to think that as they glide over the ice, they talk about the season and share their thoughts on what this joyous time of year means to them.

STONEHEARTH HUTCH, CHRISTMAS COTTAGE IV (1993) The symbols of the Christmas season speaks to us so clearly. In my *Stonehearth Hutch,* wreath and tree signal that this sunset heralds Christmas Eve. The lone, rough-hewn cottage represents the rock of faith.

VICTORIAN CHRISTMAS (1992) Some homes just beg to be painted! This stately old Victorian stands on a prominent street corner in my hometown. I decided to turn the clock back to a Christmas Eve around the turn of the century and paint the house all lit up for open-house festivities.

THE VICTORIAN GARDEN (1992) As I explored this English garden, I was struck by the overwhelming fragrance of the many blooms. Back home in California, as I worked on the final painting, I was reminded of the delightful scent.

THE BROADWATER BRIDGE, THOMASHIRE (1992) This beautiful Victorian-era stone bridge is located on an idyllic stretch of stream that was once part of a large private estate that has been converted into an exclusive trout-fishing club for gentlemen and ladies.

WEATHERVANE HUTCH (1992) My favorite detail of this tiny cottage, or hutch, is the weathervane, which depicts a plowman at work behind a draft horse. Though in my painting it is only a fraction of an inch in size, the weathervane is the cornerstone of the small cottage.

FLAGS OVER THE CAPITOL (1991) *Flags over the Capitol* is my tribute to the American spirit. Nothing brings out American pride more than a celebration with flags flying overhead and banners strung from every window. This is a time when friends, families, and neighbors join together in a spectacular display of unity and patriotism.

AMBER AFTERNOON (1992) This painting is a romantic love sonnet about the charms of the autumn season—the cooling moisture of rains and mist, and the occasional scent of burning leaves.

AFTERNOON LIGHT, DOGWOOD (1991) During my travels, as I wander around, I keep an eye out for new scenes to sketch and paint. On one of my journeys, I was walking through a village park enjoying the splendor of springtime. Everything had come to life again in a joyous display of colors and fragrances.

THE GARDEN OF PROMISE (1993) When a close friend lost loved ones, I was amazed to see the serenity and peace that filled his heart. It was almost as if, despite the hardship of parting, he was already anticipating the joyful reunion that lay ahead.

EVENING AT SWANBROOKE COTTAGE, THOMASHIRE (1992) Walking trails accompany even the smallest stream in England, and on a summer's evening a peaceful stroll beside a gently whispering brook is guaranteed to restore even the most burdened soul. On one such evening walk in England, my family and I came upon the idyllic cottage on which I based this painting.

SWEETHEART COTTAGE II A Tranquil Dusk at Falbrooke Thatch (1993) For the second work in my Sweetheart Cottage collection, I've conjured a vision of a perfect romantic hideaway. *Falbrooke Thatch* is nestled right next to a charming little waterfall, with an arched footbridge leading from the front door over the falls.

BEYOND AUTUMN GATE (1993) Some years ago, in my travels through England, I found a wonderful old stone gate—mysterious and inviting—that inspired my celebrated painting *The Autumn Gate*. Nanette and I returned to England and made a pilgrimage to that ancient gate in order to discover what lay beyond—the stately, ivy-draped stone manor house I celebrate in *Beyond Autumn Gate*.

LAMPLIGHT LANE (1993) *Lamplight Lane* portrays quaint English cottages running along a footpath, a lively stream spanned by an ornate Victorian bridge, and sunlight breaking through clouds. It seems too perfect to be real, yet I painted *Lamplight Lane* almost completely on location, at a charming little village in the English Cotswolds that looked very much like this.

HIDDEN COTTAGE II (1993) I take a great deal of pleasure in finding out-of-the-way places, small wonders that sometimes seem to go unnoticed, like the cottage behind the gate in *Hidden Cottage II.*

HEATHER'S HUTCH Sugar & Spice Cottages I (1993) Sugar and Spice Cottages is the first collection solely devoted to dollhouse cottages that any little girl would love to live in—especially one of my own daughters!

GLORY OF MORNING (1993) For me, the quality of light is delightful! Morning light is warm with the energy of a new day, yet the cool air is heavy with mist. *Glory of Morning* sparkles with the light of just such a morning – warm light filtered through myriad tiny water drops until the colors glisten.

GLORY OF EVENING (1993) *Glory of Evening* is as different from its companion piece, *Glory of Morning,* as sunset is from sunrise. The violet radiance colors the garden flowers, deepening their hues. Such glorious evenings as this lay a purple cloak upon the land . . . and every home becomes a castle.

VICTORIAN CHRISTMAS II (1993) I'm inviting you to a Christmas party unlike any you've ever attended—because it takes place a hundred years ago! In my paintings I love turning back the clock to a simpler era. That's what my *Victorian Christmas II* is all about: it brings my favorite holiday and a glorious historical period alive on canvas.

HOMESTEAD HOUSE (1993) *Homestead House* is the first painting in my Great American Mansions collection. With its stately Doric columns and imposing facade, this is the very essence of the plantation style . . . truly a grand mansion that would have delighted Scarlett O'Hara and Rhett Butler.

THE BLESSINGS OF AUTUMN (1993) *The Blessings of Autumn* begins my Blessings of the Seasons collection. Here is the fullness of autumn — the ripe orange plumpness of pumpkins, the Indian-corn wreath upon the door, the flaming reds and golds of the maples, and the soft blanket of fallen leaves.

SUNDAY OUTING (1993) A favorite family tradition of ours is the Sunday drive. After church we'll take off in the family car, often driving in California's Apple Hill country, where the neat orchards and charming old farmhouses provide a comfortable reminder that families have been enjoying Sunday outings for a long time now.

VILLAGE INN COUNTRY MEMORIES II (1993) Nanette and I are delighted to see bed-and-breakfast inns, each with its own distinctive character, becoming so popular in our own country. *Village Inn* is my dream of an intimate, utterly charming bed-and-breakfast.

ST. NICHOLAS CIRCLE (1993) I began this painting in Norman Rockwell's famous studio near Arlington, Vermont. Many charming New England cottages made their way into *St. Nicholas Circle*. In this idyllic spot time stands still, and it's Christmas all year round.

LAMPLIGHT BROOKE (1993) When I painted *Lamplight Lane* (page 93), I found myself wondering about the sylvan stream that runs alongside the village lane. *Lamplight Brooke* is my picture of what lies downstream from my original *Lamplight Lane* painting.

STUDIO IN THE GARDEN (1993) They say an artist's studio is his most important self-portrait—that's certainly true of my second studio, the romantic hideaway in the lovely village of Carmel-by-the-Sea portrayed in *Studio in the Garden*.

The Kinkade family at Ivy Gate

CHASING THE HORIZON
1993-1997

TEN YEARS AFTER THE TRANSITION from Los Angeles to Thom's hometown of Placerville, Thomas and Nanette chose to pack up the family and move to the rolling hills of a quaint village in the South Bay area of San Francisco. After moving, Nanette soon discovered she was expecting their third daughter, Winsor Christian.

 A trip to Carmel inspired Thom to envision a fantasy setting, adjacent to his home, where his studio could be built. His vision became reality, and Ivy Gate Cottage, a restored historic California bungalow, was fashioned into one of the world's most talked about studios. Less than two minutes from the family home, the studio became an art classroom for Merritt, Chandler, and Winsor, as Nanette often homeschooled the children. Thom, of course, was the art teacher.

As 1994 approached, Placerville and Carmel became meccas for Kinkade admirers. Traveling from around the United States, collectors came to Studio in the Garden, Kinkade's Carmel gallery workshop, to seek the inspiration of the artist. The popularity of his work in Carmel and Thom's enthusiasm for the area resulted in an ongoing love affair between the artist and the quaint seacoast town—he truly defined, in many people's minds, the quintessential "Carmel style" within the arts.

RETURNING SOLDIER (1996)

Thomas Kinkade called on the use of soft light and broken color as he entered into this phase of his work. Examples like *Gardens Beyond Autumn Gate*, *Blessings of Spring*, *Morning Glory Cottage*, and *Hometown Memories* presented a striking sense of color atmosphere within the context of precise detail. A new sense of subtlety and luminosity was emerging.

In the fall of 1994, the Thomas Kinkade National Archive in Monterey, California, opened to the public. There, visitors gained a historical perspective on the artist and his work. With the Archive's opening, Kinkade took a bold step in releasing impressionistic plein air images to the public in limited-edition form. As had been typical in the past, other publishers and artists were skeptical of the public's willingness to embrace nontraditional Kinkade offerings, but within four years, Kinkade dominated the art world in this genre with a record number of collectors acquiring plein air work for the first time.

A VIEW FROM CANNERY ROW, MONTEREY (1996, Plein Air) By the mid 1990s, Kinkade had begun to perfect his contemporary style of Plein Air painting with the same individuality that earned him the "Most Collected Artist" recognition. *A View from Cannery Row, Monterey* is perhaps one of the finest examples. As if Kinkade had stepped back in time to share the moment with Steinbeck himself, the artist captures the wharf atmosphere so unique to the Monterey area.

During 1996, Thom traveled with his brother, Pat, and father, Bill, through the British Isles and France, retracing the elder Kinkade's World War II adventures. The trip bonded the three men in ways that only travel can provide, and inspired a new book, *Chasing the Horizon*, published in 1997, that chronicled their escapades. Plein air works flowed from the artist during this time. It seemed impossible for Thom to travel anywhere and not capture segments of his trip through two-hour sessions with brush, paint, and easel.

Toward the end of this era, Kinkade broke free from the softer tones he had worked with over the previous three years. No two pieces speak of this transition with more authority than *Cobblestone Lane* and *Light of Peace*. *Cobblestone Lane*, with its charming English village of cottages, would be the launch of Thom's most successful series. The lighthouse masterpiece *Light of Peace* is bold in color and definition and yet presents a buttery edge that validates the artist as the romantic realist of our time. The foundation had been laid, and Kinkade's "Golden Era" would soon take form.

WAILEA POOL, MAUI (1996, Plein Air) A masterful example of Kinkade's unhibited boldness of color and texture. Painted on location on Maui, *Wailea Pool* exhibits bold, thick strokes that intrigue the viewer. This is one of the finest examples of the artist's contemporary work done spontaneously on location.

VIEW OF PUERTO VALLARTA (1994, Plein Air) In the mid 1990's, at the peak of Thomas Kinkade's emerging "on location" period of inspiration, the artist often captured subjects that were a part of a romantic getaway with Nanette. *View of Puerto Vallarta* is a typical example of this period with confident broad strokes and subtle contrast.

THE END OF A PERFECT DAY II A Quiet Evening at Riverlodge (1994) In *A Quiet Evening at Riverlodge,* second in my End of a Perfect Day collection, we visit a cozy, rustic cabin nestled in a setting rich with natural drama. Now that truly is the perfect place to end a perfect day!

MORNING GLORY COTTAGE (1995) I love flowers, I love cottages, and I love the radiant effects of morning light. In *Morning Glory Cottage,* the morning glory, a lovely vining flower, is drawn to the tranquil moods of morning light in a setting I dream of stumbling upon.

HOMETOWN MEMORIES I Walking to Church on a Rainy Sunday Evening (1995) As we stroll down the tree-shaded lane, you'll notice the landmarks familiar to every hometown — neighborhood houses, people of the village, sidewalks, and even a pet or two. This is a place where families thrive, children grow up, and memories are made.

WARMTH OF HOME (Published 1994) It will come as no surprise to you that the subject of home is near and dear to my heart, and this wilderness cabin is the essential American home.

COBBLESTONE LANE I (1996) In *Cobblestone Lane I* a path winds its way through a rustic village. The very unevenness of the cobbled walkway adds a sense of adventure that awakens our senses; we hear birdsong, feel the bracing mist of the morning, pluck a ripe apple to savor its sweet juice, smell the mingled scents, and enjoy the play of sunlight and shade.

THE LIGHT OF PEACE (1996) Storms must end. God's glorious light streams through the clouds in brilliant beams. That moment, when peace returns to the land, sea, and sky, is a wonderful affirmation. It is the inspiration for *The Light of Peace,* third in my Seaside Memories collection.

BEACON OF HOPE (1994) *Beacon of Hope* is a product of imagination and an allegory of faith. A small boat, barely visible on the horizon, rides heavy seas that surge and crash onto a rocky coast; the lighthouse beacon is the vessel's sole guide. The keeper's house is a safe haven against all storms.

SWEETHEART COTTAGE III The View from Havencrest Cottage (1994) *The View from Havencrest Cottage* anticipates a long-planned trip to the Austrian Alps. This delightful vista expresses the best of my imaginary ramblings through that romantic landscape of soaring peaks and verdant alpine valleys.

VICTORIAN CHRISTMAS III (1996) In *Victorian Christmas III* I touch the quiet heart of the holiday itself. Bowered by stately evergreens and blanketed in new snow, this golden house is aglow with the spirit of Christmas.

EMERALD ISLE COTTAGE (1994) To me, Ireland means tradition and stability — charming customs, love of family, a faith as enduring as the austere, ruggedly beautiful landscape itself. The Ireland portrayed in in *Emerald Isle Cottage* is a land rooted in the earth but touched by a heavenly light.

LAMPLIGHT INN (1994) *Lamplight Inn,* with its graceful arching bridge, invites us to make our way to its door. This spacious old country inn has room enough to welcome all weary travelers; it promises to refresh our spirits.

HIDDEN ARBOR (1994) I often seek out a quiet place to meditate and pray—a special retreat like the one in *Hidden Arbor*. This marvelous waterfall, with its myriad rivulets and streams and climbing flowers on a romantic arbor, is a little touch of heaven.

MOONLIGHT LANE I (1994) Nanette and I love to walk hand in hand in the moonlight, and *Moonlight Lane I* is our long-overdue romantic walk through the English countryside. In this painting I was particularly pleased with the way reflections of moonlight and the illuminated cottage interior mingle in the puddles.

THE BLESSINGS OF SPRING (1994) In the magical light of spring it's easy to imagine this dignified English manor house a century ago—its stately Victorian guests stepping out of their carriages to make a grand entrance amid the vibrant radiance of evening that touches the new blooms with brilliant color.

THE HIDDEN GAZEBO (1994) If you and I were to walk together along the old Plantation Road north of New Orleans, I could take you to the very spot that inspired *The Hidden Gazebo*. Perhaps the stairs that lead to the hidden gazebo will carry us to a quiet place of prayer and inspiration.

THE POWER AND THE MAJESTY (Published 1994) I like to think that water is alive with the poetry and power of God's creation. Yet, for all the awesome grandeur of the thundering falls hurtling down a sheer precipice in the *The Power and the Majesty,* I also sense a profound peacefulness that is most reassuring.

EVENING IN THE FOREST (Published 1995) I walked a sylvan stream to find the idyllic hideaway portrayed in *Evening in the Forest.* The cabin is bathed in a welcoming amber light. The wildness of wood and stream has not been tamed; it's been softened by this hint of the comfort of home.

CHRISTMAS TREE COTTAGE (1994) When I think of the glory of Christmas, I think of the radiant sunsets that set the snowy world aglow at that time of year. The luminous golden color of the sunset in *Christmas Tree Cottage* is a vibrant reminder that the glory of the season truly comes from God alone.

CHRISTMAS MEMORIES (1994) In *Christmas Memories,* first in my new series celebrating the joyous festivity of an earlier and more gracious era, one of California's great historic houses shows its festive holiday face. Colorful lights spill out from the huge Christmas tree as tethered horses await the close of festivities.

AUTUMN AT ASHLEY'S COTTAGE (1994) How fondly I remember the fragrant leaf fires that were a favorite autumn ritual of my boyhood. *Autumn at Ashley's Cottage,* with its bustling chickens in the yard and its heaps of crisp autumn leaves, delights that little boy in me.

GUARDIAN CASTLE (1994) *Guardian Castle,* my collaboration with the brilliant miniaturist David Winter, marks the first time that I've ever worked with another artist. I was captivated by David's miniature castle sculpture — so grand and regal that it seemed to call for a heroic, naturalistic landscape as its proper setting.

PARIS, EIFFEL TOWER (1994) In *Paris, Eiffel Tower,* I attempted to go beyond the topographical details of the setting and into its heart and mood to achieve my artistic goals. Bridges and buildings were moved and adjusted, and colors and lights were enhanced to capture all the delights of Paris.

SAN FRANCISCO, MARKET STREET, 1905 (1994) In *San Francisco, Market Street* I took the liberty of turning back the clock to a vivid and very colorful era. It was a time when the cable cars were an efficient way of getting around "the City by the Bay" and when Market Street was truly the heart of San Francisco.

COLLECTOR'S COTTAGE (1994) This tiny cottage, nestled beside a stream, is based on a real rustic home I discovered in the English Cotswolds. To me, it's a perfect place for friends to gather over tea and talk about favorite trips and family gatherings, about art and beauty. In short, it's the ideal clubhouse for Kinkade collectors!

BROOKSIDE HIDEAWAY (1994) *Brookside Hideaway* is my Valentine's Day gift to lovers everywhere. It's the perfect romantic hideaway, lavish with flowers . . . and on close examination you'll also find a few hearts hidden away in the distance and among the foliage. Ah, sweet love!

GARDENS BEYOND AUTUMN GATE (1994) In *Gardens Beyond Autumn Gate* a graceful Greek urn rises out of a reflecting pool, and a manor house looms above the manicured grounds. A radiant light permeates the misty air. Here is the perfection that exists only in places that touch our imaginations and our hearts.

MORNING DOGWOOD (1995) *Morning Dogwood* seemed almost to paint itself. It started its life as a plein-air impression of a tree-shaded gazebo that I saw in Hawaii. Back in my studio, I began to feel very strongly that the trees should be pink flowering dogwoods with lavish blossoms — a vision of Eden.

THE BLESSINGS OF SUMMER (1995) When I was a lad, we had our choice of Arcadian swimming holes, deep and safe, framed by old trees and big diving rocks. It was heavenly. *The Blessings of Summer,* third in my Blessings of the Seasons collection, is my tribute to those long-ago summer days.

LAMPLIGHT VILLAGE (1995) In *Lamplight Village* I wanted to create a scene with a great sense of discovery, making it seem as though you could stroll over the stone bridge and wander around the village finding things of interest everywhere you look.

THE END OF A PERFECT DAY III (1995) *The End of a Perfect Day III,* the third and final piece in my End of a Perfect Day collection, celebrates the majesty of God's creation. In the drama of sunset, the woodsman returns to his own small world — a cozy stone cabin warmed by a hearth fire and the promise of comfort at day's end.

HOMETOWN CHAPEL (1995) This is the chapel where we commemorate the milestones of our lives: the celebration of marriage, the birth of a child, the marking of an anniversary, and even the passing of a loved one. My hope is that *Hometown Chapel* will be a part of each of these milestones, shared with others as a gift.

PETALS OF HOPE The Garden of Promise II (1995) I sometimes visualize faith as a garden, where hope is in abundant bloom. In *The Garden of Promise* we stand at the gate of that wondrous retreat; in *Petals of Hope* we enter the garden where the lavish blossoms dazzle the eye and the air is fragrant with hope.

LOCHAVEN COTTAGE (1995) At twilight, a hush falls over the countryside. The wind stills, and the surface of a small lake calms to mirror smoothness, reflecting the brilliant hues of sunset. *Lochaven Cottage* welcomes us to this idyllic scene.

BLOSSOM BRIDGE (1995) I came upon a scene in Ireland where ancient footpaths wind their way over an old stone bridge to a distant village. It was all so green that I began to add brightly colored flowers . . . and suddenly a riot of colors took over.

SIMPLER TIMES I (1995) *Simpler Times I* reflects something I believe in very deeply: simplicity and the true foundations of life. My hope is that this painting will remind us of the important things, such as the enjoyment of the cycle of the seasons, the satisfaction of work and rest, and the security of family, home, and church.

AUTUMN LANE (1995) *Autumn Lane* follows a rural road into the cool depths of an autumn forest. The scene is rich with the pleasures of the season; the quiet shadows are deep, the morning light brilliant, and the turning leaves appear to be on fire.

A LIGHT IN THE STORM (1995) To those who observe with a knowing eye and an understanding heart, the natural world is rich with allegories of profound spiritual truth. *A Light in the Storm* is a visual analogy to Jesus' proclamation "I am the light of the world" (John 8:12).

STEPPING STONE COTTAGE (1995) *Stepping Stone Cottage,* second in my Sweetheart Hideaways collection, represents the refuge of my love, my family, my art, and my faith. Natural stepping stones lead across the water to the welcoming door.

DEER CREEK COTTAGE (1995) In *Deer Creek Cottage,* the world appears reborn in beauty, all the barrenness of the winter wood hidden by white. The delicate fawn, peering at the lights in the cottage windows, seems to join in the reverent mood. Perhaps even the animals of the forest can celebrate Christmas!

THE LIGHTS OF HOME (Published 1995) In *The Lights of Home* I attempted to render an epic subject on a miniature scale. The painting portrays a grandiose two-story Victorian home flanked by a rustic workshop and barn, with the farmer's fields stretching away under a blanket of snow.

ROSE GATE (1996) In the first of a trio of coordinated paintings in honor of my beautiful baby, Winsor, we enter through the floral opulence of *Rose Gate.* Two ancient stone columns guard the entrance; a weathered copper plaque bears the crest of the manor, an interlocking *W* and *M.*

WINSOR MANOR (1996) Little girls grow up to be beautiful young women. I'm beginning to see that in my own family. That's why *Winsor Manor,* the painting I've created to honor the birth of my third daughter, Winsor, isn't the charming little dollhouse cottage I painted for Merritt or Chandler. This is the romantic manor house Winsor may one day share with her Prince Charming.

LILAC GAZEBO (1996) The third in my series of paintings in honor of my daughter Winsor, *Lilac Gazebo* offers a special delight to the senses. Here the air is fragrant with the heady perfume of lilacs. This tiny architectural gem nestled in a bower of flowering lilacs is a romantic dream come true.

VICTORIAN CHRISTMAS IV (1995) This nostalgic vision of Christmas past completes one of my favorite collections, Victorian Christmas. *Victorian Christmas IV* represents a return to my personal memories. I've concentrated on family, which is, after all, the essence of Christmas.

GOLDEN GATE BRIDGE, SAN FRANCISCO (1994) I came upon a half-hidden trail overlooking the bay and followed it down through a dense eucalyptus forest leading to a small beach. A fisherman there told me, "Few know about this place, but it's like nowhere else in the world." As he spoke, a dense fog lifted, and before me stood the majestic arch of the Golden Gate Bridge.

BEGINNING OF A PERFECT DAY (1996) When a morning dawns so bright, so clear, so bursting with beauty that you can't help but pause to celebrate God's wondrous creation, that is my idea of the beginning of a perfect day.

SUNSET AT RIVERBEND FARM (1996) *Sunset at Riverbend Farm,* my first published depiction of a working farm and the initial print in my Riverbend Farm collection, is a lovely pastoral. This picture of peace and prosperity is enlivened by milling cows returning to the barn at evening, and flocks of geese and ducks that cross the pristine stream.

VENICE (1996) Venice is one of the most vibrantly romantic cities in the world. The fabulous Santa Maria della Salute provides the visual focus for *Venice*. Here are the ornate palaces, the festive sights, the wonderful gondolas that make Venice a city like no other.

HOLLYHOCK HOUSE (1996) *Hollyhock House,* second in my Flower Cottages of Carmel collection, is a painting of a real hideaway along the picturesque Pacific coast. The splendid, dignified hollyhocks, which rise as proud and straight sentinels at the entrance to the garden, are my imaginative addition to the scene.

SPRING GATE (1996) Since painting *Autumn Gate* early in my career, I've been fascinated with the inviting mystery of gates. I return to the subject, in a new season, with my heroically sized *Spring Gate.* I've portrayed a massive wrought-iron gate framed by stone pillars; it is spring, and nature rejoices at its rejuvenation with a lavish abundance of flowers.

HOMETOWN EVENING (1996) I remember wandering the lanes of my hometown on a Sunday evening, drawn as if by magnetic attraction toward the heart of the village. *Hometown Evening,* third in my Hometown Memories collection, is enriched by intense childhood memories, although I've chosen to turn the clock back a few decades.

HYDE STREET AND THE BAY, SAN FRANCISCO (1996) How well I remember riding the cable car on my first visit to San Francisco and glimpsing the magnificent panorama of the bay. I remember the famous Ghirardelli Chocolate sign, the vibrant activity on Fisherman's Wharf, the dramatic presence of distant Alcatraz Island. But most of all, I remember the magnificent bay.

HOMETOWN LAKE (1996) With *Hometown Lake*, fourth in my Hometown Memories collection, I move beyond memory to the realm of my deepest imaginings. I believe that people in every area of our nation and all parts of our culture share this vision, this longing for a peaceful lakeside place.

SUNDAY EVENING SLEIGHRIDE (1996) Snow is a wonderful mirror for moonlight, which bathes the landscape in a soft silver glow. The moon casts dramatic shadows, and under its spell, the lamps in the valley below twinkle with a special radiance.

A CHRISTMAS WELCOME (1996) Many elements of an earlier and simpler time survive in my boyhood hometown. Rustic scenes like *A Christmas Welcome,* in which horses wait patiently at a split-rail fence while their riders enjoy holiday festivities in a simple stone cottage, are treasured memories.

CANDLELIGHT COTTAGE (1996) The classic English cottage looks wonderfully warm and inviting in the glow of flickering candles. The dancing candlelight has a cozy, intimate quality — especially when it's suffused in the soft mist of this fine English evening.

MEADOWOOD COTTAGE (1996) The third painting in my Collector's Cottage series takes us to a lovely lakeside setting. Dusk has fallen, and a small wisp of smoke rises from the chimney of this quaint little stone cottage, welcoming visitors in to warm themselves by the fire and possibly partake in an evening's conversation.

LAMPLIGHT BRIDGE (1996) *Lamplight Bridge,* the fifth stop along our imaginary Brooke Windermer, is enlivened by the vibrant glitter of gas lamps. The ancient stone span, crowned by lampposts, links neighbors who dwell on either side of the stream and enhances the cozy hospitality of English country living.

HOME IS WHERE THE HEART IS II (1996) *Home Is Where the Heart Is II* expresses those things I value most about family. "Home is where the heart is" is a favorite saying of mine . . . as well as one of my favorite collections. I warmly offer this painting, heart to heart.

TEACUP COTTAGE (1997) For my wife, Nanette, the service of tea is a fascination and a fine art. I've borrowed her collection of exquisite china tea services and put it on display in *Teacup Cottage*.

PINE COVE COTTAGE (1996) I especially enjoy coastal areas where the rugged rock of the shoreline is densely covered with lush pine forest. To clear a secluded piece of ground in the forest and build a cozy stone cottage suitable for a lifetime of seaside moments is a dream I'm sure is hidden deep in each of us.

BRIDGE OF FAITH (1997) For me, the world is enriched by images of faith. In the Garden of Promise collection, I look for those moments of revelation, of joyous acceptance, that make up our common spiritual experience. Then I look out into the world to find visual images that reflect the truths of my walk with God.

THE GOLDEN ERA

1997-2000

WHEN TOM AND NANETTE CELEBRATED THE arrival of their fourth daughter, Everett Christian, it was time to search for a family van!

Commentary describing an artist's "Golden Era" is always open to scrutiny. Work done by Kinkade in 1997, however, seems to defy any argument about the use of the term. It was as if a floodgate had opened and the experience of years of sacrifice, revelation, passion, and disciplined execution was unleashed at once. In addition, Media Arts Group, Inc., Kinkade's publisher, introduced some innovative

enhancements to the limited-edition print market. Collectors could now choose from two or three different sizes of the same image. Also, limited-edition authentication was ensured by using DNA-encoded ink when

Thomas Kinkade's signature was applied to a print. Although they scoffed at this practice at the onset, other art publishers began providing similar benefits for their clients shortly thereafter.

Hundreds of art galleries representing Kinkade's work exclusively opened within a four-year period throughout the United States

A NEW DAY DAWNING (1997) *A New Day Dawning,* first in my Romance of the Sea collection, celebrates the many joyous new days that keep each of our lives vibrant and exciting — whether we are young or old, married or single. The dawn light that breaks over the surging sea recalls Paul's thrilling affirmation in Romans 13:12: "The night is far gone, the day is at hand."

and Great Britain. Eventually, Thom's cherished Cotswold countryside became the site of a Kinkade gallery housed in a beautiful 1600s thatched-roof cottage. Collectors visited Kinkade galleries in large malls and obscure hamlets all over the United States, Canada, and Europe, lured by the message and artistic mastery of Kinkade's work.

The so-called Hall of Fame releases from 1997 appeared to be a launching pad, not a destination. Many of the published artworks were recognized by the National Association of Limited Edition Dealers as back-to-back award winners, including *New Day Dawning,* *Clearing Storms, Beyond Spring Gate, Valley of Peace, Village Christmas, Cobblestone Brooke, Garden of Prayer, Bridge of Faith*, and *Hometown Lake.* If there had been a barrier, Thom broke through it with this incredible collection.

In 1998, Kinkade offered up a Norman Rockwell tribute in *Holiday Gathering*, inspired by an earlier trip to Rockwell's Arlington, Vermont, studio. Thomas continued the tradition of honoring

Rockwell in future work as well. Kinkade presented other milestones in his career during the next three years. *Quiet Evening*, *Stairway to Paradise, Mountain Chapel*, and *Forest Chapel* represent a cross section of the offering. Kinkade called on his impressionistic talent as he went to work on *Boulevard Lights*, a Paris street scene. Art collectors could see the influence of Edouard Cortez on the modern-day master. The crowning touch for Kinkade's cherished city scenes would be presented in *Carmel, Sunset on Ocean Avenue*, released in 1999. It was as if he had taken his finest traits and brought them together for all to enjoy. Note the street painter!

Thom entered 2000 with an interpretive rendering of Placerville. *Hometown Morning*, with its paperboy hard at work, harks back to his teenage courtship years with Nanette.

It was during this era that the artist was encouraged to release a little-known work that had been an art school project. Offered as *Prince of Peace*, Kinkade's portrait of Christ was appreciated by his collectors late in its release. Today, it has become one of his most sought-after works.

CLEARING STORMS (1997) *Clearing Storms* is a symbolic scene charged with a joyous message. Storms — dark, brooding, terrifying — are a part of our lives. When we're in the grip of a storm, we may feel abandoned by God. The meaning of *Clearing Storms* is that God's love is eternal.

BEYOND SPRING GATE (1997) In spring, the song of new life fills the air and thrills our hearts. Every blooming gate promises to lead us into a paradise where love and peace prevail. In *Beyond Spring Gate,* the second in my Spring Gate collection, I try to fulfill that promise by leading my collectors to a vernal paradise.

THE VALLEY OF PEACE (1997) *The Valley of Peace* marks the first time I featured the golden beauty of aspen trees in my mountainscapes. Nature has her garden spots; this is one of them. Here, truly, is a perfect retreat for the dreamer who lives in all our hearts.

VILLAGE CHRISTMAS (1997) In *Village Christmas,* I tried to capture a Christmas of a simpler place, where streetlamps glow with the warm light of a natural flame and the townsfolk use a leisurely stroll to church as an opportunity to stop and chat about the joyous season.

COBBLESTONE BROOKE Cobblestone Lane II (1997) *Cobblestone Brooke* is inspired by Castle Combe, located in England's Wiltshire District. Nanette and I discovered this charming village during our wanderings over the British countryside and fell in love.

THE GARDEN OF PRAYER (1998) Perhaps in a garden we are closer to our Creator. We certainly are closer to His creation. My prayer is that this painted garden will be a meeting place for many that would speak to their God.

TWILIGHT COTTAGE (1998) The subject of *Twilight Cottage* is more than a charming little cottage nestled by a stream. It is nothing less than the joyful melody of cricket song and cascading water, the romance of sunset enhanced by a silvery sliver of waning moon—in short, the peace that passeth understanding.

STILLWATER BRIDGE (1998) The cooling, tranquil feeling of resting beside still waters . . . what trouble or pain could not be hushed by such a moment? *Stillwater Bridge* is an attempt to portray waters that are still and inviting. I hope you can linger a moment or two.

GARDENS BEYOND SPRING GATE (1998) All of us, I believe, carry a memory of Eden. Life began in that garden, and for me, many of the good things in life are still to be found in gardens. When I came upon the blooming Spring Gate, I accepted its invitation to explore — partly to satisfy a secret longing for the splendid gardens I expected to discover within.

A HOLIDAY GATHERING Christmas Cottage IX (1998) Of all the holiday rituals, the one I prize the most is the coming together of loved ones in shared celebration. Even if our family circle is small, the Christmas season can become a benchmark of friendship, a time when we pause to savor traditions of comfort and joy.

HOMETOWN BRIDGE (1998) My Hometown Memories collection fondly revisits my idyllic childhood, and I have often found that the heart and emotions of the boy seem to blend with the mind and sensitivities of the adult artist. As a maturing artist, I recognize deeper meaning within bridges, those ravine-spanning passages we make in life: graduations, first love, marriage, the birth of a child.

THE WIND OF THE SPIRIT (1998) The wind, too, has its work to do. The windmill harnesses the freedom of the wind — a biblical symbol for the unfettered spirit — to the ponderous purpose of the millstone. Fleecy clouds and delicate V's of geese trace the wind's comings and goings.

STAIRWAY TO PARADISE (1998) There are earthly places, living moments that speak to the deepest part of my imagination. They offer a glimpse of paradise on earth. In *Stairway to Paradise* a classic stone stairway, embraced by climbing roses and shaded by lavish flowering plum and dogwood trees, is such an emblem of the eternal.

THE MOUNTAIN CHAPEL (1998) Before we ever began to build temples in His honor, God graced us with natural sanctuaries radiant with the light of divine love and peace. As my Chapels of Nature collection unfolds, we will seek the presence of God in His lakes, forests, hills, and valleys.

MOUNTAIN MAJESTY (1998) *Mountain Majesty,* the third and concluding print in my Beginning of a Perfect Day collection, expresses the harmony of man in nature that can make life supremely satisfying.

EVERETT'S COTTAGE (1998) Perhaps a family is like a garden—each child a delicate rose that with the nurturing of a gardener can flourish and bring beauty to the world. Our newest little "bloom" is our daughter Everett. On her first birthday, I present this garden, and this cottage, in her honor!

CARMEL, OCEAN AVENUE II (Study, 1998) An artist's colony on the central California coast, Carmel welcomes millions of tourists each year to its beaches and village life. Ocean Avenue announces newcomers to this small village, just one mile square. If you listen carefully at night, you can hear the crashing surf and the call of the sea lions in the distance.

CARMEL, SUNSET ON OCEAN AVENUE (1999) Ten years before, I had painted *Carmel, Ocean Avenue on a Rainy Afternoon*, and from the day I finished it, I dreamed of working on a second view of the famous scene. *Carmel, Sunset on Ocean Avenue* is that long-awaited painting. A luminous sunset bathes the entire scene in a warm glow, as though a tranquil moment has been frozen in time.

LAKESIDE HIDEAWAY (1999) I certainly hope that those who follow my art will recognize elements of the good life as I have often tried to portray it when they see *Lakeside Hideaway*. This tranquil lake, nestled in the shadows of a towering mountain and next to a cozy cabin snugly lit for evening, is certainly my idea of life at its best — the perfect hideaway for heart and soul.

THE SEA OF TRANQUILITY (1998) How true it is that we often sail to distant shores seeking that which lies hidden in our own heart, our own home. *The Sea of Tranquility* does not represent a place; it is all places, for it is buried deep within all people.

SUMMER GATE (1999) Every gate has its season. The season for this dramatic portal, with its monumental pillars and ornate ironwork, its lavish blossoms and delicate palette of floral colors, is clearly summer. *Summer Gate* introduces my third print series to embrace the promise of a season by exploring the enticing world that lies beyond a secluded gate.

THE OPEN GATE (1999) *The Open Gate* is based on a real location in the English Cotswolds. I've kept the sketch for years, waiting for the perfect occasion to use it. I've found it now. This unassuming portal, perhaps a half-forgotten side entrance to the gardens, is left open as an invitation to all. Will your childlike heart inspire you to journey forward?

THE PRINCE OF PEACE (Published 1999) In 1980, as an art student, I came to have a personal relationship with Christ. Awash in my newfound faith, I was sitting in an art class, my mind wandering. As I went through the motions, my eyes on the disinterested model posing for the class, I was suddenly struck with a powerful vision. The vision that was laid on my heart that day is the painting you see before you, *The Prince of Peace.*

SUNRISE (1999) I truly believe that this millennium will come to be characterized as the "Millennium of Light," and I pray *Sunrise* will be symbolic of a new dawning of God's grace and love in the years ahead.

THE FOREST CHAPEL (1999) *The Forest Chapel* portrays a daydream I've had many times. Often, while hiking some wooded trail, I'll come upon a spectacular flowering meadow and think, What a wonderful place to worship God. The Holy Spirit dwells in the chapel and in the glade that houses it. Both proclaim the presence of God.

BOULEVARD LIGHTS, PARIS (1999) I'm a great believer in the importance of first impressions. That's one reason *Boulevard Lights, Paris* is so dear to me; it's the first print in my City Impressions collection. The City of Lights was a springboard to my imagination even before the first of my many visits there.

EVENING MAJESTY (1999) The real star of *Evening Majesty*, first in my Beginning of a Perfect Evening collection, is the luminous sunset. To my mind, this would be the perfect place to curl up by the fire.

POOLS OF SERENITY (1999) It may be that all of us carry in our souls a memory of Eden. That could account for the attraction I've long felt for gardens. *Pools of Serenity* speaks to those personal associations . . . and to something more. I've reached into the core of my spiritual life to express what I can only call the wonderfully comforting friendship I feel with my God.

CONQUERING THE STORMS (1999) In *Conquering the Storms,* sixth in my Seaside Memories collection, I confront images of God's awesome power — lightning, storm clouds, driving winds, pounding surf. Here in truth, is a storm that can shake us to the core of our being. But if we hold on to the rock of our faith, we can ride out any storm.

EVENING GLOW (1999) In 1990 when I launched my decade-long celebration of the season with *Christmas Cottage,* I had no clear idea of the challenges ahead. As I close it with *Evening Glow,* I can tell you I also had no idea of the pleasures that awaited me.

FOXGLOVE COTTAGE (1999) An artist has a duty to follow his muse — even when it leads him down unexpected or inconvenient paths. I live by that rule, and sometimes I'm rewarded with a lovely treasure like *Foxglove Cottage* — newest in my Flower Cottages of Carmel print collection.

A PEACEFUL TIME (2000) The gifts of love are beyond compare, and chief among them is a peace that passeth understanding. Domestic tranquility, as it fills a home to overflowing and permeates the world, is the subject of *A Peaceful Time,* second in the trio of prints conjuring images of very special places in the heart.

HOMETOWN MORNING Hometown Memories VI (2000) *Hometown Morning* is the sixth and final look at my boyhood hometown. I see it as a beginning, rather than an end. After all, I met my future wife, Nanette, on my paper route. And for me that was the beginning of all good things.

YOSEMITE VALLEY Study for *The Mountains Declare His Glory* (2000) Driving the old Yosemite Valley ring road, I found myself in a familiar spot. I brought my paint and canvas onto that inspiring boulder and, in little more than an hour of feverish work, created *Yosemite Valley*. A powerful insight struck me as I carried the canvas to my car: these mountains are nothing less than an image of God's grace. So returning to my studio, I used my *Yosemite Valley* study as a foundation for a major studio composition, *The Mountains Declare His Glory*.

THE MOUNTAINS DECLARE HIS GLORY (2000) After completing my recent plein-air study of Yosemite Valley, the mountains' majesty refused to leave me. I began to imagine how it might feel to live in perfect harmony with such grandeur, to be literally a part of the valley. As a final touch, I even added a Miwok Indian camp along the river as an affirmation that man has his place, even in a setting touched by God's glory.

LAMPLIGHT MANOR (2000) In *Lamplight Manor* a Celtic cross adorns a massive chimney, while a sheltered old gazebo provides a tranquil retreat for worship. Here we can anticipate the glory that awaits the children of God in heaven.

COBBLESTONE BRIDGE (2000) Recently, Nanette and I explored a new corner of the British Isles: the Hampshire region in southwest England. As we walked its quaint paths, I felt a longing for a time when rambling was a preferred mode of transportation. In the world of *Cobblestone Bridge,* man and nature live in God's perfect balance.

LIGHT OF FREEDOM

2000-2004

THOMAS KINKADE would usher in the new millennium with his family beside him. The children were old enough to travel, and that was just what the family did over the next few

years. Thom was invited to the White House in celebration of America's first Christmas of the new millennium. Nanette and the girls accompanied him with the First Family on a tour of "the nation's house." Kinkade presented the president with his rendering of the White House at Christmastime, *The Lights of Liberty*.

Within the year, Kinkade traveled again to England, where he and Nanette were invited to Queen Elizabeth's banqueting hall during the Queen Mother's hundredth birthday celebration. Sixty Kinkade artworks were on display under the murals painted by Rubens. The epic release *Cobblestone Bridge*, inspired by a diversionary trip to the Cornwall region of England, was announced at the event. It was apparent that all of the artist's skills had come together in one voice in this new work. Hundreds of guests attended the spectacular gala, bringing Kinkade and his artwork to the attention of European collectors. Residents of the northern United Kingdom particularly appreciated the recognition Thom gave his ancestral Scotland.

THE LIGHT OF FREEDOM (2002) For *The Light of Freedom* I turned once again to my faith in God, my love for my fellow man, and my pride in America and what it stands for. Now is the time when each of us must summon courage and strength so that the light of freedom will forever illuminate this glorious country. God bless America.

Tragedy struck the United States in September of 2001 with the terrorist attacks on the World Trade Center in New York and the Pentagon in Washington, D.C. Kinkade, moved by the heroism of those who responded to New Yorkers in need, sought a way in which he could contribute. Inspired by a dream, Thomas executed an emotional rendering that, as he stated, was God-given. Painted during three days of little sleep, Kinkade's *Light of Freedom* became his contribution to an ailing nation. Thom and the family flew to New York to present the artwork to firemen and police officers. Using the painting, the Salvation Army raised millions of dollars for relief.

Like most people, Thomas Kinkade is, in part, a personality shaped by a lifetime of experiences. It goes without saying that events of the first years of the millennium had an effect on the work that followed. Serious in his nature, Thom began work on his next cityscape masterwork. He called on the city that had inspired him many times before. *San Francisco, Lombard Street* delivered just the right subject matter for this time in his life: grand architecture that was also a bit on the whimsical side.

Lombard Street may be considered one of Kinkade's best-known achievements. Yet today he continues to create the unexpected. *Streams of Living Water, Almost Heaven, Cobblestone Mill, Clock Tower Cottage, Moonlit Cottage, Peaceful Retreat, Village Lighthouse* — each piece is a product of the artist's twenty-year journey, brought forward as a contemporary vision.

Kinkade's day often begins at seven A.M. and ends ten to twelve hours later. One might think his recent work *Perseverance* is an image of the artist, unwilling to cease, triumphant over the storm. The storm for Kinkade may be the endless quest for excellence in his work and respect for those who have gone before him.

Thomas Kinkade's recent masterwork *New York, 5th Avenue* may well be honored as the finest Kinkade painting yet. We will know soon enough. The collectors vote by comments made as they buy the work and hang it on the walls of their homes and offices. History tells us one thing: We have yet to scratch the surface of Kinkade's enormous creative reserves. If we ask the artist, "What is your favorite Kinkade painting?" Thom would most assuredly say, "The next one."

Surely, the best is yet to come.

A PERFECT YELLOW ROSE (2001)
Nanette has always been especially fond
of roses, and yellow roses are a token of
our love. As I applied the radiant pigment
to *A Perfect Yellow Rose,* I was reminded
again of the love that has filled my life
with blessings.

THE ROSE GARDEN (2001) As a playful gesture of love, I've dedicated this lavish "rose garden"
to Nanette and our four beautiful daughters—the five most precious "blossoms" in my garden.
The Rose Collection continues with two companion paintings—detailed studies of individual red
and yellow roses to flank this Edenlike setting.

A PERFECT RED ROSE (2001) The red rose
is the flower of passion. It is the rich scarlet
of our heart's blood. *A Perfect Red Rose* is
the emblem of the greatest love of all. As
such, it also represents the human love that
so enriches our lives—of man for woman, of
parent for child.

VICTORIAN LIGHT (2000) When I began to paint this imposing lighthouse, I was lost in reverie. What would it be like, I wondered, if the keeper's house were more than the humble cottage that met my eyes? What if, instead, it matched the tower in grandeur and dignity? Here, in *Victorian Light,* is the wonderfully civilized formal grace of a great mansion married to the primal strength of a light tower.

MOONLIGHT COTTAGE (2000) In *Moonlight Cottage* I celebrate the enchanting moment when the moon begins to appear above a sheltered cottage set within a forest. Beholding this scene as the sounds of the forest envelop you and the moist fragrance of evening fills your lungs would be a transcendent moment. I cannot imagine a more peaceful experience.

PERSEVERANCE (2000) In *Perseverance* thunder crashes, sails billow, waves toss the fragile boat. We see that the clouds are about to break. The seas will calm; the sailor's perseverance will soon be rewarded with a return to God's safe haven. Perhaps this painting can assure each of us that if we can simply persevere, God's hand of love will soon disperse each storm.

COBBLESTONE VILLAGE (2000) *Cobblestone Village* seems a century removed from what we typically find in our fast-paced culture. English country life is slow, rich, and satisfying. Activity centers on the village to an extraordinary degree. The gathered townsfolk in *Cobblestone Village* are as natural and as informal as the overgrown hedges of flowers that line the lane.

STREAMS OF LIVING WATER (2000) The stone walls of the chapel seem to grow out of the earth itself, while the pristine waters of the stream cascade in the distance. Deer, birds, rabbits, and even a frog gather in humble and silent witness to the unity and harmony of the creation. And over all, the glorious vault of the heavens unfolds another glistening morning.

CLOCKTOWER COTTAGE (2001) *Clocktower Cottage* is a multifaceted allegory encompassing many dimensions of time. The painting is itself a time traveler, carrying with it a message memorialized for generations to follow: Your stay on earth is brief; consider the days and be wise.

ROCK OF SALVATION (2001) I was struck recently by the gospel music phrase "rock of salvation" and suddenly felt myself challenged to present it in one of my prints. *Rock of Salvation* is the last creation in my Seaside Memories series. Though watching the sun set over this seven-year collection of works is nostalgic and slightly bittersweet, I look forward to the sunrise of a new coastal series in the near future.

THE GOOD SHEPHERD'S COTTAGE (2001) *The Good Shepherd's Cottage* is an allegory in paint, an image of the Lord returning to call in His faithful. His house is an utterly comfortable and secure cottage, radiant with light. The air is luminous with sunset; the sound of His voice thrilling as He calls His sheep into a verdant meadow.

IT DOESN'T GET MUCH BETTER (2001) When you stumble on a breathtaking fishing hole like this on a mist-drenched morning, it hardly matters whether they're biting or not. When, as in my very hopeful canvas, the stately fisherman, properly outfitted in full waders, hooks on to a feisty rainbow trout, it truly doesn't get much better than this.

OLYMPIC MOUNTAIN EVENING (2001) The thing that most excites me about the Olympics is the inspiring fusion of age-old tradition and cutting-edge technology inherent in each competition. How fitting that the millennium's first Olympics should take place in the American West, where the past continuously informs and defines the future.

A PERFECT SUMMER DAY (2001) My new Celebration of the Seasons collection will visit four perfect days, each of which expresses the essence of its time of year. The theme of *A Perfect Summer Day* is the exuberant fullness of life. *A Perfect Summer Day* is a tapestry, woven in honor of this most joyful of God's seasons.

THE ASPEN CHAPEL (2001) A grove of aspens high in the mountains would be an idyllic place for worship. I have imagined just such a place in *The Aspen Chapel,* where aspen trees shimmer in the breeze like liquid gold.

MEMORIES OF CHRISTMAS (2001) Christmas is the season of light, and the hue that permeates *Memories of Christmas* is the rosy glow of sunset. The nostalgic vision of life is often described as "seeing the world through rose-colored glasses." This celebration of community, set in simpler times, is perhaps best viewed through such tinted lenses!

THE SEASON OF GIVING (2001) *The Season of Giving* embodies the very essence of Christmas — a celebration of charity and renewed hope. Likewise, these two sentiments form the cornerstones for the very mission of the Salvation Army.

BEYOND SUMMER GATE (2001) Summer is the season of color. The full range of nature's rainbow hues is on display in this floral paradise. In *Beyond Summer Gate* I've compressed the season, allowing the early-flowering dogwood and the late-blooming azalea to display their brilliant blossoms together. The tranquility of evening has settled on this country manor, inviting us to stroll the grounds before we settle in for some tea and talk. I hope you will join me.

SPLIT ROCK LIGHT (2001) I am intrigued by lighthouses. Erected in locations of great peril, they often stand in settings of remarkable beauty and drama. Where nature is most powerful, it can also be most majestic.

SAN FRANCISCO, LOMBARD STREET (2001) This is a golden evening; the warm glow of sunset banishes the mist and paints the busy street with its cheerful light. The exuberance of city life is evident everywhere. On Lombard Street, on an evening such as this, life is a gala celebration of the endless possibilities of city life. I invite you to celebrate with me.

THE HOUR OF PRAYER (2002) An hour spent in meditation provides a glimpse of eternity. We look to the garden of prayer for such sweet repose, and in *The Hour of Prayer,* I believe we find it. The painting anticipates the dawning of a peaceful kingdom when time will be no more and prayer will be a direct communion with the divine.

THE VILLAGE LIGHTHOUSE (2002) *The Village Lighthouse* portrays a village nestled into a rocky shore that I discovered on a seaside stroll in England. A radiant glow bathes the village, touching the magnificent flowering dogwood and lavish stands of foxgloves and impatiens with light, just as it illuminates the waves that dance over the ocean. Wisps of spray rise from the waves while plumes of smoke ascend from the chimneys. Land and sea, man and nature, are in perfect harmony here.

CAPE HATTERAS LIGHT (2002) When the sun sets, the lighthouse reveals its purpose. Though no longer in operation, Cape Hatteras Light still stands—a reminder of God's eternal vigilance on our behalf. *Cape Hatteras Light* celebrates the generosity of God's bounty as revealed in His sunsets and the serene strength of His loving guidance, symbolized by this historic lighthouse.

LILAC COTTAGE (2002) *Lilac Cottage,* the fourth issue in the Flower Cottages of Carmel collection, is inspired by a real cottage I discovered amid an overgrown garden in Carmel. When I painted *Lilac Cottage,* I searched for what I can only call the "look of lilac" and found it in the shimmering morning mist that seems unique to California.

ALMOST HEAVEN It Doesn't Get Much Better II (2002) The fisherman seems insignificant among so much grandeur; yet he is intensely a part of the scene. Like him, we are at once humbled and exalted by immersion in nature. I would take everyone with me on my fishing expeditions if I could. And, indeed, through my art, I hope that I can transport you to where it is almost heaven.

DESERT SUNSET (2002) Looking over the vastness of the desert at sunset, I was struck by how the twinkling of the distant lights looked like a glittering necklace of diamonds and pearls upon a velvet cloth. I've long admired the vast vistas, intense silences, and almost spiritual solitude of the desert. I'm not sure why it's taken me so long to celebrate those qualities on canvas; I hope to return to them soon.

PATHWAY TO PARADISE (2002) *Pathway to Paradise* continues on a spiritual and artistic journey toward a vision of the sublime. We find ourselves wandering a pathway that winds through wonders of nature—lavish, rainbow-hued blossoms—that affirm the promise of God's love. I like to think of myself as a fellow discoverer on the pathway to paradise—I invite you to travel this glorious road with me.

HOMETOWN PRIDE (2002) Bathed in the golden light of late afternoon, the scene in this painting conveys the simplicity and serenity of life in everyday neighborhoods across America. Old Glory flies over the scene, reflecting the glorious light of sunset in its red, white, and blue. As you gaze down the sun-drenched lanes and past the picket fences, my prayer is that you will envision a summer afternoon in your hometown.

COBBLESTONE MILL (2002) The mill wheel will turn for as long as the stream that powers it flows, grinding the flour that sustains a simple, satisfying village life. Beauty—and all else that is good—is a gift of light bestowed by the sun, which also grows the grain that will be ground in this mill. *Cobblestone Mill* reminds us that all blessings flow timelessly from the hand of God.

A PEACEFUL RETREAT (2002) Like you, I spend my time in a world more complex than the one I imagined in *A Peaceful Retreat*. But it is good, sometimes, to retreat, at least in our imagination, to a quiet place where one can refresh and restore the soul. In that spirit, I invite you to share with me the tranquil pleasures of *A Peaceful Retreat*.

SWEETHEART GAZEBO (2003) For me, *Sweetheart Gazebo* represents a modest palace of love. At once intimate and expansive, private and open, this most romantic shelter shows the dual nature of love. The image of romance would not be complete without a reminder of God's grace, which is the foundation on which all human love rests. The stream brings the gift of pure water to the garden, just as divine love nourishes the loving heart.

HOMETOWN CHRISTMAS (2002) I find that the places I feel most at home in share a sense of neighborhood, streets and gathering places where people come together in good fellowship and are warmed by the light of love during that preeminent celebration of home and family—the Christmas season. I've gone to special lengths to make *Hometown Christmas* a personal celebration of your favorite place, wherever in this glorious land it may be.

NEW YORK, FIFTH AVENUE (2003) Now more than ever, New York is America's city—a symbol of our indomitable spirit, our energy, our roots in a proud past, our confidence in the future. I've intentionally made this a timeless image of New York, as two-wheeled hansom cabs and classic American automobiles patrol the busy streets. The essence of the great city, as the essence of the country it so nobly represents, remains the same throughout decades past and into the future.

SEASIDE HIDEAWAY (2003) *Seaside Hideaway* evokes the rapture Nanette and I feel when we are alone together. The cottage hideaway is enveloped in flowers and graced by climbing roses—the lavish palette of sunset paints the cottage as well. Warm lights gleam through the myriad windows; we can imagine the cozy, congenial scene within.

LILAC BOUQUET (2003) My challenge in *Lilac Bouquet* is to convey the sensual experience of the garden. I want my viewers to delight at the delicate contrast of mauves and purples, to sense the rich perfume of lilacs wafting on the breeze, to imagine the buzz of bees hovering around the flowers. *Lilac Bouquet* extends my celebration of this regal and fragrant shrub; it is, in effect, a companion to *Lilac Gazebo*.

BRIDGE OF HOPE Bridges of Inspiration I (2003) The bridge in *Bridge of Hope* is as sturdy as the massive granite flagstones that form its arch and will stand for as long as the quicksilver brook rolls down from the hills beneath it. A magnificent white dogwood, a symbol of the purity of God's grace, shades the bridge. The tree's overarching boughs remind us that while we stand on the "bridge of hope," we are enshrouded by the loving embrace of our Creator.

AMERICA'S PRIDE (2003) *America's Pride,* the first piece in my new Flags over America collection, features the same dramatic sky and waving flag seen in my previous painting *The Light of Freedom,* while below I pay tribute to the most patriotic of all American cities—our nation's capital.

ABUNDANT HARVEST (2003) In *Abundant Harvest*, I savor the fruitfulness of God's creation as it is revealed in a lush vineyard estate in California's Napa Valley, where grape vines laden with fruit embrace the charming gazebo and balloons dance in the breeze.

BLESSINGS OF CHRISTMAS (2003) *Blessings of Christmas* takes a fresh look at the charming cottage of *Victorian Garden II* in its evergreen bower in the snowy grip of winter. Somehow, the warmth of family life lived in this cozy dwelling is accentuated by the shroud of snow that sits so gracefully on the trees. The cheerful snowman wrapped in his red scarf and wielding a straw broom embodies the very spirit of the season.

THE OLE FISHING HOLE, CHILDHOOD MEMORIES I (2003) I'm sure that my affection for the simple pleasures of life stems from my memories of growing up in the little town of Placerville, roaming the California foothills with my friends, savoring the freedom and security of my boyhood, dreaming the dreams of childhood and having so many come true. I celebrate my own Childhood Memories with *The Ole Fishin' Hole*. Covered bridges like this one were rarities in the Sierra foothills, but it seemed, at least in my boyhood imaginings, that big trout gathered in their shadowy depths. My faithful dog was the perfect companion for splendid summer adventuring.

PLEIN AIR

Steeped in the history of the French Impressionists, Thomas Kinkade would bring his studio from inside to the outdoors. Plein Air painting (painting "in the open air") developed in the little village of Barbizon, just outside of Paris, during the nineteenth century. Although many give artists like Degas, Renoir, and Monet the credit for developing the Plein Air movement, it would be the quest for honesty on canvas by masters like Millet (later viewed as a Realist) that inspired artists to capture their subject in a moment of time with natural light and color. California artists like Edgar Payne would further the movement of Plein Air painting and captivate Americans during the early twentieth century with his renderings of majestic panoramas of the West.

Thomas Kinkade is at home in the great outdoors. A world traveler, with brush, paint, and easel, Kinkade presents a master's touch to his admiring collectors through broad strokes and bold colors. The continents of the globe have become this artist's studio.

SEASIDE VILLAGE (1998)

CAPITOLA BEACH (1993)

TOWER BRIDGE, LONDON (1998)

GARDENER'S RETREAT (2001)

ISLAND AFTERNOON, GREECE (2000)

THE ROBERT GIRRARD
COLLECTION

Kinkade was heavily influenced by the French Impressionists early in his career, so he felt using a French-sounding pseudonym would be appropriate when he painted Impressionist works. With the name Robert Girrard, Thomas Kinkade found a new identity.

The eighties was an exciting period in Girrard's career, solidifying him as an American Impressionist master. "I wanted to reinvent academic styles—implementing my own use of light. Impressionism was an avenue that beckoned that pursuit."

In the early 1980s, Girrard began exhibiting his original oil paintings in the highly competitive and well-publicized Carmel, California, art market. His scenic, Impressionistic paintings met with immediate success. The sophisticated use of broken color yields a soft atmospheric effect on his canvases.

SILVER AND GOLD (Published 2002)

RADIANT SURF (Published 2002)

INDEX
OF PAINTINGS